LED ZEPPELIN

YOU SHOOK ME

CAT NO: BZB0261

Photography courtesy Pictorial Press, Wikimedia
Commons, Getty Images unless indicated otherwise.

Made in EU.

ISBN: 978-0-9930170-0-1

Contents

The year was 1966, and popular rock music was at a crossroads. One month The Beatles were - according to John Lennon - "bigger than Jesus", and then the next they were performing their last ever official concert. Surf rock was at an all-time high, as Pet Sounds by the Beach Boys took the world by storm, and Simon and Garfunkel's Sounds of Silence topped the Billboard charts. Heavy rock, however, was an unknown quantity; an unknown quantity, that is, until a young, talented guitarist from Heston in Middlesex joined forces with the likes of Jeff Beck and Eric Clapton in the British rock quintet The Yardbirds.

That guitarist, of course, was Jimmy Page, the future founder of British rock stalwarts Led Zeppelin, and the forefather of heavy metal. This is his, and Led Zeppelin's, formidable story...

After originally joining The Yardbirds as a bassist, Jimmy Page soon switched to second lead guitar, creating a powerful, duelling frontline attack with Jeff Beck, who went on to form both Jeff Beck Group and Fusion. In a promo interview in 1999, Page talked of his blues-inspired early years with The Yardbirds as being one of the main reasons the chemistry of Led Zeppelin was so special, stating, "I think it was that we were really seasoned musicians. We had serious roots that spanned different cultures, obviously the blues. I was seduced by R&R as a teenager and that's what made me want to play. From then I discovered the blues and country blues, folk musicians, then folk with Arabic and on and on. I was gobbling it all up, then it just came up as the music that you heard."

When Beck left the group in 1966, The Yardbirds were beginning to wind down. Page had designs on forming a supergroup with both he and Beck on guitars, and The Who's drummer Keith Moon and bassist John Entwistle also canvassed as possibilities. Steve Winwood, Steve Marriott and Donovan were also being lined up as potential lead singers. In spite of an early 1966 recording session with Page, Moon and Beck, the group failed to materialise, although future Led Zeppelin bassist and synths man John Paul Jones was also involved in the recording session, which touched upon early Indian influences. In an interview with Dave Schulps of Trouser Press in the summer of 1977, Jimmy Page said of the experience, "In those early days I was very interested in Indian music, as were a lot of other people too. Most of the "textbook" of what I was forced to learn was while I was doing sessions, though."

The Yardbirds played their final gig in the summer of 1968. However, with obligations to play several concerts in Scandinavia, Page and bassist Chris Dreja took up the band's name to fulfil the dates. Recruiting Birminghamborn singer Robert Plant and fellow Midlander John Bonham on drums, the band looked all set to play the gigs, until, that is, Dreja opted out of the mproject to become a photographer. Nevertheless, Page quickly contacted John Paul Jones, who agreed to join the band as bassist. The band completed the Scandinavian tour as The 'New Yardbirds'. The seeds had been sown. Led Zeppelin were about to take the world by storm...

Originally the Led Zeppelin name had been conceived for the Beck/Page supergroup, as Page recounted in his 1977 Trouser Press interview, "We were going to form a group called Led Zeppelin at the time of "Beck's Bolero" sessions with the lineup from that session. It was going to be me and Beck on guitars, Moon on drums, maybe Nicky Hopkins on piano. The only one from the session who wasn't going to be in it was Jonesy, who had played bass. Instead, Moon suggested we bring in Entwistle as bassist and lead singer as well." Keith Moon himself had come up with the name from John Entwistle's term for a bad gig, which he described as "going over like a lead zeppelin". The 'a' of 'lead' was dropped to prevent "thick Americans" from pronouncing it "leed".

Securing an advance deal with Atlantic Records in the winter of 1968 (incidentally the largest ever advance paid to a rock band at the time), Led Zeppelin made its U.S. concert tour debut in Denver within a month, before moving on to dates in Los Angeles, San Francisco, and other west coast cities. In the same Jimmy Page interview with Dave Schulps in 1977, Page spoke of his excitement at having both Plant and Bonham in the group: "When I auditioned him and heard him sing, I immediately thought there must be something wrong with him personality-wise or that he had to be impossible to work with, because I just could not understand why, after he told me he'd been singing for a few years already, he hadn't become a big name yet. So I had him down to my place for a little while, just to sort of check him out, and we got along great. No problems. At this time a number of drummers had approached me and wanted to work with us. Robert msuggested I go hear John Bonham, whom I'd heard of because he had a reputation, but had never seen. I asked Robert if he knew him and he told me they'd worked together in this group called Band Of Joy."

Shortly after this first foray into America for Zeppelin, the band released their self-titled debut album in January of 1969. On recording the album in almost record time, in 1999 Jimmy Page recalled, "I think it comes out to 36 hours - I

know that because I had to pay the bills. It wasn't like we went into there for 36 hours non-stop, but we paid for 36 hours of studio time. We had a chance to air the songs onstage in a small tour of Scandinavia. It gave us a change to know the number before going in the studio. JPJ and I were veterans in the studio so we had all the discipline. John Bonham and Robert had been in the studio before for a couple of things. It wasn't like anyone was going in there for the first time. Everyone got swept away by the energy of it," Blending elements of folk, distorted amplification, Eastern sounds and, in particular, blues, Led Zeppelin was one of the pivotal records in the pioneering of the heavy metal movement of the 1970s.

Included on the album were cover versions of I Can't Quit You Baby, by legendary bluesman Willie Dixon, and You Shook Me, by Dixon and J.B. Lenoir. Page later said of the influence of blues, "As far as the blues, it just captured them hearing Chicago blues. When the Stones first started they were doing really good interpretations of Muddy Waters songs and all that Chess catalogue. They weren't the only ones, of course. Down in the South (London), that's what was going on. Then you had the Beatles in Liverpool with "Please, Mr. Postman", and it really wasn't the same deal as what was going on down South, but it got very popular and changed what was going on. It wasn't so much, for me, their music, but the fact that they wrote their own songs and all of a sudden they opened the door for any band that could write songs. I started doing studio work. That's the big change they made on the music scene."

The album, in spite of receiving mostly favourable reviews, also famously started a long-running feud between Led Zeppelin and Rolling Stone, after John Mendelsohn, journalist for the magazine, savaged the band for mimicking black artists, 'over-riffing', and straight-out stealing compositions. Marking the beginning of numerous rejections from the band for interviews and cover stories with the magazine, as their level of success escalated, Robert Plant said in interview with Rick McGrath in 1971, "...things like Rolling Stone get out of hand. Even in England people buy it because it's been around for such a long time. It gets to be a habit. And what they read is something else, man. Because it's always down, down, down. Why don't they stop all that and start being nice? Is that such a hard thing to do?"

More controversy came about after Led Zeppelin's Hindenburg disasterbased album cover earned the band a threat of legal action from a relative of the creator of the Zeppelin aircraft. Whilst the short-lived legal activity was still in the air, the band, hilariously, changed their name to The Nobs.

Still, it wasn't all gloom and doom, as Led Zeppelin's live shows began to gain quite a reputation, as Lester Bangs from Rolling Stone testified in November, 1970, describing their sound as a "..thunderous, nearundifferentiated tidal wave of sound that doesn't engross but envelops to snuff any possible distraction."

Off the back of Led Zeppelin I's success, the second album - Led Zeppelin II - gained similar notoriety late in 1970, reaching number one on both sides of the Atlantic. The album included more alleged plagiarism, with songs strikingly similar to work by Willie Dixon, in particular, provoking a lawsuit against the band from Arc Music. Jimmy Page spoke of the band's copying in his interview for Trouser Press in the summer of 1977, stating, "The thing is they were traditional lyrics and they went back far before a lot of people that one related them to. The riffs we did were totally different, also, from the ones that had come before, apart from something like "You Shook Me" and "I Can't Quit You," which were attributed to Willie Dixon. The thing with

"Bring It On Home", Christ, there's only a tiny bit taken from Sonny Boy Williamson's version and we threw that in as a tribute to him.

People say, "Oh, 'Bring It On Home' is stolen." Well, there's only a little bit in the song that relates to anything that had gone before it, just the end." Page has also been quoted as saying, "I've often thought that in the way the Stones tried to be the sons of Chuck Berry, we tried to be the sons of Howlin' Wolf."

In terms of reviews, former Led Zeppelin enemy number one John Mendelsohn described Led Zeppelin II as a "heavyweight" of an album, adding that the niche the band had carved out for themselves through the long player was both "distinctive and enchanting".

During this early period in their career, Led Zeppelin made numerous tours of America. As their popularity grew they moved on from clubs and small ballrooms to larger concert halls. Sometimes lasting over three hours, these gigs would include plenty of improvisation, soul- and funk-based interludes, and ridiculously long drum solos from John Bonham. It should come as no surprise that due to the nature and majesty of these shows, many have been preserved as Led Zeppelin bootleg recordings.

For their third studio album, Led Zeppelin III, Jimmy Page and Robert Plant made the remote cottage in Wales, Bron-Yr-Aur, their spiritual and recording base. Thanks to the less hectic atmosphere the resulting album was more of an acoustic affair than previous outings, and was strongly influenced by Celtic music. During an interview that took place post show in San Diego in the summer of 1977, Jimmy Page spoke of the decision to record the album in the cottage, and the effect that it had on the album, stating, "After the intense touring that had been taking place through the first two albums, working almost 24 hours a day, basically, we managed to stop and have a proper break, a couple of months as opposed to a couple of weeks. We decided to go off and rent a cottage to provide a contrast to motel rooms. Obviously, it had quite an effect on the material that was written."

The band's newly acquired acoustic sound received mixed reactions from critics. Lester Bangs from Rolling Stone, for example, stated in a review of the album from late 1970 that it "doesn't challenge anybody's intelligence or sensibilities", and that the acoustic sound is merely "standard Zep graded down decibelwise."

This negative media reaction didn't pass the band by; as Jimmy Page himself stated, "Well, it got some bad press. That's something we should talk about later. But there was an incredible wave of Led Zeppelin mania, or whatever, and we had just finished a very successful tour, and then the album came out and nothing happened." He added, "I just thought they hadn't understood it, hadn't listened to it. For instance, Melody Maker said we'd decided to don our acoustic guitars because Crosby, Stills and Nash had just been over there. It wasn't until the fourth LP that people began to understand that we weren't just messing around."

Still, over time the album has gained a more positive reputation, and is now generally praised. In an interview with Robert Plant taken in 1971 by Rick McGrath in Vancouver, Canada, Plant explained the importance of 'going acoustic': "...that album was certainly a large step after the second one. Because you can't keep turning out the same thing. If you do that, you can't do anything for yourself. We know we can rely on things like Whole Lotta Love and it is quite easy to work within the same framework all the time. But who does that? Just people who haven't got anything going for them in the brains, that's who. And I think the third album

was an essential thing, I don't care if it sold any copies at all, because it showed there was a bit more attached to us and it than Shake Your Money-Maker sort of stuff."

As well as the music, Led Zeppelin III was also noteworthy for its unique album cover. Featuring a wheel which, when rotated, displayed various images through cutouts in the main jacket sleeve, it came as a perfect example of the band's innovative and artistic nature; a nature they held so dear, in fact, that they were loath to do anything by the book at all, resisting television appearances, shunning music interviews, and being vehemently opposed to releasing singles. Jimmy Page explained this somewhat strange behaviour in an interview with Trouser Press' Dave Schulps in the late 1970s, when talking of gigging Led Zeppelin III, "I felt a lot better once we started performing it, because it was proving to be working for the people who came around to see us. There was always a big smile there in front of us. That was always more important than any poxy review. That's really how the following of the band has spread, by word of mouth. I mean, all this talk about a hype, spending thousands on publicity campaigns, we didn't do that at all. We didn't do television. Well we did a pilot TV show and a pilot radio show, but that's all. We weren't hyping ourselves. It wasn't as though we were thrashing about all over the media. It didn't matter, though, the word got out on the street."

The relative success of Led Zeppelin's early years was dwarfed by a fiveyear period in the 1970s in which the band released their biggest-selling albums, changed their image to be more befitting of the era, and took part in many of rock's most infamous tales of excess and debauchery. This was Led Zeppelin at their most musically successful, and their most rock and rolling excessive. As Rick McGrath, a Canadian interviewer, simply stated in 1971, Led Zeppelin were "the seminal heavy metal band of the early 70s", with

Robert Plant being "The Frontman" and Jimmy Page "the definitive guitar hero of his age. Describing a concert in Vancouver in the same year, he talks of the "Zepheads" who would travel the length and breadth of the country to see the band's "zany" show. Led Zeppelin were, figuratively, on top of the world.

This isn't to say that everybody 'got' the band during this time. In a review of the group's Maple Leaf Gardens Concert from the summer of 1971, Jack Batten of the Globe & Mail attacks the band from all angles, describing Robert Plant's stage posturing as narcissistic, Jimmy Page's guitar-playing as "depressingly antiquated", and the music itself as "good music to get stoned by".

Still, the band roared on and on, as the group's fourth studio outing was just about to be released to both massive critical and fan response. Speaking about the recording process, Robert Plant recollected, "We finished that, and we did it in our own home. Well, how it went was that we used a mobile truck for our recording unit and we went to an old manor in Surrey. There we put up all the equipment in one room and stuck all the mike leads through a window. Straight into the recording van. So anything that we did just went straight down on tape. Bit by bit it grew up into a great collage of numbers."

Hitting the stands on November 8, 1971, Led Zeppelin IV came out with no indication of either a title or band name on the original cover, but instead four symbols were printed on the LP, one for each of the band members. Once again, the reason for this was the band's disdain for the critics who had labelled them as being over hyped, and had criticised the third album as being a lesser effort than their previous two albums. Wanting to prove that the music could sell itself without any indication of the band's name, Led Zeppelin IV was

thus released in this anonymous way. Speaking of the cover with Dave Schulps of Trouser Press in San Diego in 1977, Jimmy Page explained the band's decision, stating, "After all this crap that we'd had with the critics, I put it to everybody else that it'd be a good idea to put out something totally anonymous. At first I wanted just one symbol on it, but then it was decided that since it was our fourth album and there were four of us, we could each choose our own symbol. I designed mine and everyone else had their own reasons for using the symbols that they used."

The album itself further refined the band's unique formula of combining folky, acoustic elements with both blues and heavy metal. The critics lapped it up, with Dave Schulps of Trouser Press pronouncing, "The fourth album was to my mind the first fully realized Zeppelin album. It just sounded like everything had come together on that album."
In a first for the band, album track "Rock and Roll", a tribute of sorts to the early rock and roll music of the 1950s, albeit with that famed Led Zeppelin heavy metal twist, was the first ever Led Zeppelin song to be licensed for use in advertising, being used in Cadillac commercials as of 2006.

As well as this, the folk- and metal-infused epic "Stairway to Heaven" became a massive radio hit in spite of never actually being released as a single. In fact, in America alone, in its full thirty-five years of existence, Stairway to Heaven has amassed an incredible fifty years' worth of radio airplay - a full FIFTEEN years longer than the track has actually been out for!

Jimmy Page himself attributed a good portion of the album's success to Robert Plant's newfound songwriting skills, stating of "Stairway to Heaven" in particular, "I always knew he would be, but I knew at that point that he'd proved it to himself and could get into something a bit more profound than just subjective things. Not that they can't be profound as well, but there's a lot of ambiguity implied in that number that wasn't present before. I was really relieved because it gave me the opportunity to just get on with the music."

It has often been speculated that "Stairway to Heaven" masks hidden Satanic messages, and allegedly when played backwards these messages can be heard. The band themselves have always vehemently denied these claims, but this speculation, along with the fact that Page dabbled in the occultist writings of Aleister Crowley, gained the band a lot of bad publicity during this time. Also, "Stairway to Heaven", once again, was jumped on by the critics for its somewhat similar riff to the track "Taurus" by American rockers Spirit, for whom Led Zeppelin had opened on their first American tour.

Led Zep, however, maintained that the resemblance was purely coincidental. Mostly, however, for this album the critical response was good. Lenny Kaye of Rolling Stone remarked in the December 23, 1971 issue of the magazine that the album was "remarkable for its low-keyed and tasteful subtlety", and that Page's arranging and producing was "some of (his) tightest". As well as this, in 2005 Guitar World magazine held a readers' poll in which "Stairway to Heaven" was voted as having the greatest guitar solo of all time. As of the summer of 2006, Led Zeppelin IV had sold 23 million copies in the United States, making it the third-best selling record in the history of the American music industry. Worldwide, it ranks at number eleven for album sales. Many people, including Guitar World, pinpointed Page's guitar playing as being the main reason for the album's success, with Page responding to this praise by saying, "Without a doubt. As far as consistency goes, and as far as the quality of playing on a whole album, I would say yes. But I don't know what the best solo I've ever done is - I have no idea. My vocation is more

in composition really than in anything else. Building up harmonies. Using the guitar, orchestrating the guitar like an army - a guitar army."

The band's fifth studio album, Houses of the Holy, was released in 1973, and further enhanced the band's love of experimentation, featuring longer tracks with the expanded use of synthesisers and multi-layered guitar symphonies in tracks such as "No Quarter" and "The Song Remains the Same" respectively. The album also features a couple of compositions from John Bonham, something that hadn't surfaced on the previous four albums.
The album also featured a couple of 'comedy' tracks in "The Crunge" and "D'yer Maker"; as Dave Schulps of Trouser Press tells of the band's newfound 'sense of humour', "There are a few tracks on the fifth album that seemed to exhibit more of a sense of humor than Zeppelin had been known for. "The Crunge" was funny and "D'yer Mak'er" had a joke title which took some people a while to get." The album topped the charts, and the subsequent tour across the United States broke numerous records for concert attendances, including Tampa Stadium in Florida, where Led Zeppelin played to almost sixty thousand fans, breaking the record set by The Beatles at Shea Stadium in 1965. Three sold-out shows at Madison Square Garden in New York were filmed for a Led Zeppelin film, The Song Remains the Same, that would be released in 1976.

In terms of reviews, the album was another relative critical success. In spite of "The Crunge" and "D'Yer Mak'er" (pronounced "Jamaica" - get it?) being hailed as the band's most tenuous efforts to date, the rest of the album was well received. Gavin Edwards of Rolling Stone magazine gives credence to the album, yet prophesies the band's eventual decline, stating, "...eventually excess would turn into bombast, but on Houses, it still provided inspiration." It seemed, in many ways, that the real backlash had begun - the same way it would with Oasis, Blur, and any other popular outfit nearly thirty years later.

The album was to be the band's last with their record company, as Led Zeppelin launched their own record label, Swan Song, in 1974 as a vehicle to promote their future albums. As well as promoting themselves, the band would also expand the label's roster to include such acclaimed artists as Pretty Things, Midnight Flyer and Bad Company. Jimmy Page said of the band forming their own label after Houses of the Holy, "We'd been thinking about it for a while and we knew if we formed a label there wouldn't be the kind of fuss and bother we'd been going through over album covers and things like that. Having gone through, ourselves, what appeared to be an interference, or at least an aggravation, on the artistic side by record companies, we wanted to form a label where the artists would be able to fulfil themselves without all of that hassle."

In the mid 1970s both sides of the Atlantic were hit by the emergence of punk. Blues-inspired heavy metal was on the decline, and Led Zeppelin began to feel inspired to pick things up, as bassist John Paul Jones stated in an interview with D.A. Miserandino in the late 1990s, "Punk kind of woke us up again. 'Oh yeah, I remember what we are supposed to be doing here.' It was about to go for a change of gears and round two."

In an attempt at something of a riposte to the punk movement, the group released their first ever double album. Hitting the stands on February 24, 1975, Physical Graffiti was also the band's first release on their new record label. Consisting of fifteen tracks spread out over two LPs, eight tracks were recorded at Headley Grange in 1974, with the remaining tracks having been recorded years

previously, but not released on earlier albums. Varying wildly musically, Physical Graffiti included Eastern influences, Indian influences and Arabic influences to name but three. Speaking of the nature of the album in a promotional interview from 1999, Jimmy Page stated, "It's the whole light and shade of the band. When you say 'heavy metal' it's the intensity of the riffs, really. There's some majestic music like Kashmir' - some music that can really caress, like 'Ten Years Gone'."

Reviewed by Jim Miller in Rolling Stone magazine in the spring of 1975, Physical Graffiti was referred to as Led Zeppelin's "bid for artistic respectability", adding that there was no real competition for the band when it came to being the world's biggest rock band, with only The Rolling Stones and The Who as real contenders for the crown. Still, in spite of this, Physical Graffiti was a massive critical and commercial success, and showed that in spite of the rise of punk, Led Zeppelin still had what it took to be a big band in an ever-increasing market place. In fact, not only was Physical Graffiti a success in its own right, but it also helped increase sales of previous releases, with all preceding albums simultaneously re-entering the Top 200 Album chart shortly after its release.

Embarking on yet another record-breaking U.S. tour after the album's release, it barely seemed important that the likes of Jim Miller were noting that the new album contained "no startling breakthroughs", and that Led Zeppelin were "not the greatest rock band of the Seventies."

Only a couple of months later the band played to five sold-out crowds at Earls Court in London, footage from which would surface in 2003 on the Led Zeppelin DVD. So ethereal were the concerts, in fact, that they were widely considered to be some of the best of the band's career.
By the mid 1970s Led Zeppelin were one of the biggest

names across both Europe and North America. Selling out concerts and record stores, left, right and centre, the band perpetually topped the charts on both continents. With their live shows steadily growing in artistry and theatrics, the band continued their commercial and critical success right up until 1980. However, terrible misfortunes such as the 1977 death of Robert Plant's son, Jimmy Page's increased heroin use, changing musical tastes both within the band and in the music industry in general, and, finally, John Bonham's death in 1980, would finally bring an end to Led Zeppelin. This, if you will, is how it all went wrong... Following their fine performances at Earls Court, the band were forced into some unscheduled time off as the first of many tragic events occurred for Robert Plant. Whilst on holiday in Greece, Plant and his wife Maureen were involved in a serious car crash that left Plant with a broken ankle, and Maureen with injuries so serious that a blood transfusion only just managed to save her life. Unable to tour due to the state of Plant's health, the group instead went back into the studio to record what would be their seventh album - Presence.

Recorded in Munich, Germany, and released in March 1976, the album marked a massive change in the Led Zeppelin sound, moving away from hard rocking electric anthems balanced with acoustic ballads and complicated arrangements, to a more straightforward, guitar-based affair enhanced with punk-like riffs and a much more aggressive arrangement.

Easily the heaviest album in the Led Zeppelin back catalogue, Presence showed signs that the band were succumbing to the punk invasion, and almost embracing the sound with open arms. The haunting vocal work from Plant is even more striking when you consider that it was done almost entirely from his wheelchair as he slowly recovered from the aforementioned car accident. Talking

about the recording of the album in an interview with Dave Schulps of Trouser Press magazine in June 1977, Jimmy Page announced, "As far as living it uninterrupted from beginning to end, yeah, definitely. I did 18-hour sessions, 24-hour sessions to complete it."

Despite the album being another massive commercial success, critically it received a rather mixed response. Stephen Davis of Rolling Stone gave the album one of its more admirable reviews, stating that it confirmed the group's "status as heavy-metal champions of the known universe", adding that "Presence is another monster in what by now is a continuing tradition of battles won by this band of survivors." Others, however, saw differently, with Dave Schulps questioning the production values of the album, pronouncing, "I think it was just a reflection of the total anxiety and emotion at the period of time during which it was recorded. It's true that there are no acoustic songs, no mellowness or contrasts or changes to other instruments." Others still went further, dismissing it as sloppy, and questioning whether the band's now legendary excesses may now have caught up with them, for the recording of Presence coincided with both John Bonham's extreme alcoholism, and the beginning of Jimmy Page's heroin use.

A double-edged sword, since Plant's ankle injuries prevented the band from touring in 1976, it did give them a chance to finally get some wellearned rest, as well as completing the concert film The Song Remains The Same, along with its soundtrack album. As it was the only official live documentation of the band available prior to the BBC Sessions being released in 1997, Dave Schulps of Trouser Press enquired as to the nature of the concert movie in a June 1977 interview with Jimmy Page, with Page stating, "...it was an incredible uphill struggle. We'd done a bit of work on it and stopped, did more, then stopped again. Three times in all. At that point, we'd decided to redo the thing, making sure the filmmakers did have everything

covered properly. As far as it goes, I'm really pleased that it's there. Purely because it's an honest statement, a documentary. It's certainly not one of the magic nights."

The film itself was recorded over three nights of concerts at Madison Square Garden in 1973, during the Houses of the Holy tour. Far from being 'just another concert', each member of the band filmed a unique 'fantasy sequence' to be shown during a particular song. For the sake of completeness, Plant's sequence involved rescuing the classic damsel in distress; Page's depicted an Aleister Crowley and occult-inspired moonlight ritual; Jones' featured an enormous, overblown pipe organ; and Bonham's presented a number of speeding cars. Premiering in October 1976, the band finally came together once again to perform on tour in 1977, embarking on another U.S. concert tour, selling out venues all over the country.

Once again the tour was a massive fiscal and musical success; however cracks were beginning to show off-stage. On June 3 1977, a gig was cut short at Tampa Stadium due to a severe thunderstorm, which caused a riot to break out in the audience, ultimately broken up by police with tear gas. The resulting mess included numerous injuries and arrests. The following month, after a July 23 show at Oakland-Alameda County Coliseum in California, John Bonham and members of the band's management team were arrested after an affiliate of promoter Bill Graham's Oakland concert staff was badly beaten during the performance. Rumour has it that the beating took place after said member of staff allegedly slapped Led Zeppelin's manager's son when he was spotted taking down a dressing room sign. When Led Zep's manager, Peter Grant, heard about this he went into the trailer along with Bonham and security officer John Bindon, and beat the man senseless.

To top it all off, real tragedy struck the following day after the group's second Oakland concert, as news came in that Plant's five-year-old son, Karace, had died from a stomach virus. The rest of the tour was immediately cancelled, and this proved to be the last date the band would ever play in the United States.

Throughout this period various members of the band had been at loggerheads with each other, with Page and Bonham generally recording their album parts separately from Plant and Jones, with Jones stating in an interview with D.A. Miserandino that, "You don't hang around when you're not working. When you are working, you're really pleased to see each other. That's how it was. Bands like Traffic - who all lived in the same house - by the time they got on the road they were at each others' throats. They were ready to kill each other, whereas we were all friends. It was a cycle of touring and being close and having that time off. It was a great cycle."

This new album was, of course, In Through the Out Door, and would prove to be the band's final studio album. Recorded in the latter part of 1978 and throughout 1979 in ABBA's Polar Studios in Stockholm, Sweden, In Through the Out Door featured a mass of experimentation, as the band seemingly moved towards the synth-led music age with little to no difficulty. The album topped the charts on both sides of the Atlantic, and actually became the first rock album to debut in the number one spot on the American Billboard Album Chart. Charles Young of Rolling Stone magazine would describe the release as being driven, mainly, by "Bonham's exuberance" on the drums, as well as Plant's rather inane, but largely successful, lyrical prowess. Praise for Page, however, was less forthcoming. Whether it was due to his excessive use of heroin during this period, or whether he had just lost interest in the band, Page's creativity was described as "failing", and because of this "even Led Zeppelin was no longer Led Zeppelin".

In August 1979, Led Zeppelin headlined at Knebworth. The huge music festival proved to be a massive success, with close to 120,000 fans witnessing the partial return of Led Zeppelin. Still, the sparkle had gone, and Robert Plant was not particularly eager to tour full-time again, and was even considered leaving the band. Persuaded to stay on by manager Peter Grant, a low-key European tour was arranged for the summer of 1980, featuring stripped-down sets, with lengthy solos, jams, and drum interludes conspicuous by their absence.

On June 27, in Nuremberg, Germany, the concert came to an abrupt halt after John Bonham collapsed on stage in the middle of the third song. Quickly rushed to hospital, this was the beginning of the end for Bonham, who would be dead less than three months later. With ever-mounting speculation in the press that Bonham's demise was due to excessive use of drugs and, in particular, alcohol, on this occasion it turned out that he had simply eaten too much, and had had a severe case of heartburn! Returning to the stage only a couple of nights later, Bonham and the rest of the band completed the tour, and were all done and dusted by July 7, in Berlin. Plant, and the group as a whole, were enthusiastic about the prospect of touring again, and plans for a large American tour were made for that autumn - a tour that, unfortunately, would never come to fruition.

On September 24, 1980, Led Zeppelin assistant Rex King picked up John Bonham to attend rehearsals at Bray Studios for the planned autumnal tour of America - the band's first major tour since 1977. During the journey Bonham had asked to stop for breakfast, where, Bonham being Bonham, he downed four quadruple vodkas (equivalent to 2/3 pint) along with a solitary bite of a ham roll. Continuing to drink the second he hit the studio, the band continued playing until late in the evening before making their way to Jimmy Page's house in Windsor.

According to sources, just after midnight Bonham fell asleep and was carried to bed. Since he had drunk a total of over forty shots that night, John Paul Jones and tour manager Benji LeFevre went to check on Bonham the following morning, only to find him dead. He was 32 years old.

The cause of death was asphyxiation from vomit. A subsequent autopsy found no other substances in Bonham's body, so it was the alcoholism that had plagued his career from the very early days of Led Zeppelin that led to his premature demise. John Bonham was cremated on October 10, 1980, at Rushock in Worcestershire. He has since been well remembered by all and sundry, including Jimmy Page, who recalled in an interview in 1999, "Almost the moment he died, they put him in Playboy as one of the greatest drummers, which he was - there's no doubt about it. There's never been have to hear a live performance to see the way he could approach things and his imagination was far beyond any other drummer that I've ever played with."

Rumours of a replacement joining the group came thick and fast, with the likes of Cozy Powell, Carmine Apple, Bev Bevan and Simon Kirke all bandied around as possibilities. The remaining band members, however, felt that they couldn't carry on without Bonham and disbanded Led Zeppelin soon after his death. They issued a joint press statement on December 4, 1980, which once and for all confirmed that the band would not continue without Bonham behind the drums: "We wish it to be known that the loss of our dear friend, and the deep sense of undivided harmony felt by ourselves and our manager, have led us to decide that we could not continue as we were."

In 1982, Page, Plant and Jones released a final record of sorts, through a collection of out-takes of various sessions throughout the band's career. Coda, as it was to be called, also included two tracks taken from Led Zeppelin's performance at the Royal Albert Hall in 1970, as well as other studio sessions. Kurt Loder of Rolling Stone described the album as "a resounding farewell from the greatest heavy-metal band that ever strutted the boards", adding that the track selection is a "marvel of compression, deftly tracing the Zeppelin decade with eight powerful, previously unreleased tracks, and no unnecessary elaboration." He finished by describing the album as "a classy way to go out."

Having essentially hung up his guitar following Bonham's death, Jimmy Page eventually picked it up again to embark upon a short charity tour for multiple sclerosis is 1983. Touring alongside former The Yardbirds guitarists Eric Clapton and Jeff Beck, Page was almost back to where he started, and was fast regaining his love of music - so much so, in fact, that in 1984 Page worked alongside Paul Rodgers (formally of Free and Bad Company) and brought out two albums under the name The Firm, the first of which included a composition originally intended as a Led Zeppelin track. At the same time Robert Plant was also embarking on his own solo project - and a successful one at that - with the 1982 album Pictures at Eleven. In mid 1984 Plant and Page teamed up once again to record the highly successful EP The anybody since. He's one of the greatest drummers that ever lived. You only have to hear a live performance to see the way he could approach things and his imagination was far beyond any other drummer that I've ever played with."

Rumours of a replacement joining the group came thick and fast, with the likes of Cozy Powell, Carmine Apple, Bev Bevan and Simon Kirke all bandied around as possibilities. The remaining band members, however, felt that they couldn't carry on without Bonham and disbanded Led Zeppelin soon after his death. They issued a joint press statement on December 4, 1980, which once and for all confirmed that the band would not continue without

Bonham behind the drums: "We wish it to be known that the loss of our dear friend, and the deep sense of undivided harmony felt by ourselves and our manager, have led us to decide that we could not continue as we were."

In 1982, Page, Plant and Jones released a final record of sorts, through a collection of out-takes of various sessions throughout the band's career. Coda, as it was to be called, also included two tracks taken from Led Zeppelin's performance at the Royal Albert Hall in 1970, as well as other studio sessions. Kurt Loder of Rolling Stone described the album as "a resounding farewell from the greatest heavy-metal band that ever strutted the boards", adding that the track selection is a "marvel of compression, deftly tracing the Zeppelin decade with eight powerful, previously unreleased tracks, and no unnecessary elaboration." He finished by describing the album as "a classy way to go out."

Having essentially hung up his guitar following Bonham's death, Jimmy Page eventually picked it up again to embark upon a short charity tour for multiple sclerosis is 1983. Touring alongside former The Yardbirds guitarists Eric Clapton and Jeff Beck, Page was almost back to where he started, and was fast regaining his love of music - so much so, in fact, that in 1984 Page worked alongside Paul Rodgers (formally of Free and Bad Company) and brought out two albums under the name The Firm, the first of which included a composition originally intended as a Led Zeppelin track. At the same time Robert Plant was also embarking on his own solo project - and a successful one at that - with the 1982 album Pictures at Eleven. In mid 1984 Plant and Page teamed up once again to record the highly successful EP The Reuniting at Live Aid in the JFK Stadium in Philadelphia, Page, Plant and, now, John Paul Jones, played alongside Tony Thompson and Phil Collins to a pretty average fanfare. As well as the uneven, out of time

drumming from both Thompson and Collins, the band's performance was malso marred by Page's badly tuned guitar and Plant's atypically poor vocal performance.

In spite of Jones giving the group some credibility, when footage of the concerts was released in 2004, the band unanimously agreed not to allow footage of that particular performance to be used, conceding that it was far from their usual high standards. Following their work with Thompson, it was decided that the band would reform with the drummer in the spring of 1986. Gathering in the south of England for rehearsals, the band were all set to spread their creative wings once more.

It clearly wasn't meant to be, however, as a near-fatal car accident involving Thompson soon put paid to the group's plans. After 1986's false start, 1988 proved to be a significant year for the surviving Led Zeppelin members, with much talk of a reunion tour. These rumours were enhanced, in part, by Plant's appearance on Page's album Outrider, and Page's appearance on Plant's solo album Now and Zen, one track of which featured samples of Page's guitar riffs taken from original Led Zeppelin recordings. As well as this, for the first time since Bonham's death eight years previously, Robert Plant began performing Led Zeppelin songs on his solo tour, and when Plant's European tour hit London in the spring of 1988, Jimmy Page joined Plant on stage for several songs. It came as no surprise, then, that Led Zeppelin did indeed reunite in the May of 1988, for Atlantic Records' 40th Anniversary Concert, with John Bonham's son, Jason, on drums. Still, as at Live Aid three years earlier, the performance was a flawed one, in part due to Page's oddly understated performance, and by a lack of synths in the mix. In 1989 the band performed with Jason Bonham once again, this time at the 21st birthday party of Plant's daughter, Carmen, as well as performing at the 1990 wedding of Bonham himself. As is only right and true, these performances caused much speculation in the media about a possible Led Zeppelin reunion tour, though no such tour ever materialised.

Moving into the 1990s, it had been ten years since John Bonham's death, and there seemed to be little chance of the band coming back together again to record any new material. In the summer of 1990, Page, once again, joined Plant on stage for a brief set at Knebworth. Including three Led Zeppelin numbers, the performance proved to be one of the highlights of the event, and was broadcast all over MTV. On other dates of Robert Plant's tour to promote his new album, Manic Nirvana, Plant sported a Jimmy Page t-shirt, and revelled in performing Led Zeppelin tracks by the dozen. The love of the band's music was still clearly there for all to see, as John Paul Jones himself noted in an interview with D.A. Miserandino in the late 1990s, stating, "Lately, there's been a resurgence of interest in the band, The BBC Sessions. And it seems the whole popularity got an entirely new breath of life."

Not that Jones' relationship with Page and Plant seemed to be a particularly healthy one, as there were discordant times ahead in the mid 1990s. Page and Plant again reunited in 1994 for a Led Zeppelin MTV Unplugged performance. Crudely dubbed 'Unledded', the performance eventually led to a rather grandiose world tour with a Middle Eastern orchestra, as well as a live album entitled No Quarter. The bass player for the Unplugged session and subsequent tour was not actually John Paul Jones, but was in fact Charlie Jones, who had been Plant's bassist for many years now, and was also his new son-in-law, having married Plant's daughter, Carmen. Essentially Page and Plant had begun touring without so much as a by-your-leave from Jones, and tensions were further increased when, after being asked at a press conference where John Paul Jones was, Robert Plant jokingly replied, "parking the car." Jones then went

on to add more fuel to the fire by stating he was unhappy that the live album had been named after a Led Zeppelin track which had been largely his own work, and in a 1995 interview with Spin magazine, Jimmy Page even went so far as to kick an interviewer out of the room for even mentioning Jones. The gloves were clearly well and truly off.

On January 12, 1995, Led Zeppelin were inducted into the grandly titled United States Rock and Roll Hall of Fame. At the ceremony itself, the rift between Page, Plant and John Paul Jones was split wide open when, upon receiving his reward, Jones none-too-subtly jested, "Thank you, my friends, for finally remembering my phone number!" causing more than a little discomposure and a few awkward looks shared between Robert Plant and Jimmy Page. Performing together at the show, the three played alongside another couple of old rock crooners, in the form of Aerosmith's "toxic twins", Joe Perry and legendary set of lips Stephen Tyler, on three Led Zeppelin and two Neil Young numbers.

A relatively quiet spell followed, before Atlantic Records released a single edit of Led Zeppelin II's "Whole Lotta Love" for the American market. Worthy of note as the band's one and only CD single, additional tracks on the release included "Baby Come On Home" and "Travelling Riverside Blues", in what proved to be a precursor, of sorts, for the November 11 release of Led Zeppelin's BBC Sessions. The first Led Zeppelin album in more than fifteen years, since 1982's Coda, BBC Sessions was a two-disc set including almost all of the group's admirable recordings for the BBC.

In 1998, Plant and Page continued their lengthy collaboration with Walking into Clarksdale, an album consisting of entirely new material - the pair's first together since Led Zeppelin's disbandment. A subsequent album

tour also featured Led Zeppelin songs aplenty, as well as tracks more than a little influenced by the heavy metal forerunner's epic sound. In the autumn of 1999, Jones also joined the fray, by releasing his debut solo album, Zooma, which he followed up in 2001 with The Thunderthief.

Neither made much of an impression on either side of the Atlantic. In October 2002, the hyenas of the British press reported that Robert Plant and John Paul Jones had finally shaken hands and reconciled after the twenty-year feud that had kept Led Zeppelin apart since Coda. Once more, rumours surfaced of a 2003 reunion tour, and once more the rumours remained unfounded, as Plant and Page's management company denied all knowledge.

Living in the retro-loving times that we do, 2003 saw a resurgence in Led Zeppelin's popularity with the release of live album How the West Was Won, as well as a video collection, Led Zeppelin DVD, both featuring masses of material from the group's glory days. By the end of the year, the DVD had sold over half a million copies. More glory followed the following year, when in Christmas 2004, "Stairway to Heaven" was voted the best song of all time by Planet Rock listeners in a poll conducted on the station's website. As mentioned earlier, the track is also the most played track in American radio history. As well as "Stairway to Heaven", "Whole Lotta Love" and "Rock and Roll" also made it into the station's Top 10 list.

In 2005, as is right and true, Led Zeppelin received a Lifetime Achievement Award at the Grammy's, as well as being ranked number one on music TV's VH1 show 100 Greatest Artists of Hard Rock. Also in this year, readers of highbrow music magazine Guitar World voted the guitar solo in "Stairway to Heaven" the best guitar solo of all time, and Jimmy Page was, somewhat unfairly, ranked the ninth best guitarist of all time in Rolling Stone magazine, who

also voted Led Zeppelin as the fourteenth-Greatest Artist of All time. Finally, to finish off the year, it was announced in November of 2005 that Led Zeppelin and Russian conductor Valery Gergiev were the winners of the 2006 Polar Music Prize, with the King of Sweden presenting the prize to Page, Plant and Jones, along with John Bonham's daughter, in Stockholm in May of 2006.

As we move toward the current time, it is clear that the band are as revered now as they ever were. On the cover of the February 2006 issue of Guitar World magazine Led Zeppelin were proclaimed "the world's greatest band." Featured in the magazine numerous times over the years, Led Zeppelin, and Jimmy Page especially, have been cited as a major influence for an incredible amount of musicians, and in 2006, Led Zeppelin IV was named the number one guitar album of all time by a voter poll in the October issue of the magazine.

Slated to appear at the Montreux Jazz Festival on June 30, 2006, Page and Plant unfortunately had to cancel, after Jimmy Page pulled out citing medical problems. However more honours followed, as in 2006 Led Zeppelin were once again inducted into a hall of fame, this time the UK Music Hall of Fame. Australian rockers Wolfmother performed "Communication Breakdown" as a dedication to the band at the ceremony, and Megadeth's album release of this year features a cover version of Led Zeppelin's "Out on the Tiles". The band continue to shine and shine, in spite of not recording a studio album since the late 1970s.

And, as for the future? Well, Led Zeppelin, like ABBA, has always been very protective of its back catalogue. It used to be a rare occurrence when a film or TV commercial was allowed to use a Led Zeppelin track, but in recent years the band has softened somewhat, with Led Zeppelin tracks being used in the likes of Fast

Times at Ridgemont High, Dogtown and Z-Boys, Almost Famous, and Jack Black's School of Rock. Still, the band are somewhat apprehensive about letting their songs be used for commercial projects, unlike 1960s and 1970s rock contemporaries The Who and The Rolling Stones, whose tracks are seemingly bandied around everywhere. In spite of the increasing need for bands to make their back catalogues available for online music downloads, Led Zeppelin still steadfastly refuse to do so, a position which is unlikely to change in spite of the ever-growing market, showing that the band are as stubborn now as they were when they had their feud with Rolling Stone magazine at the very beginning of their career.

Has any British band had as much impact on the face of rock and roll music in America, Europe, the world as a whole, in the twentieth century, as Led Zeppelin has? Well, it's arguable - you could consider Oasis, Black Sabbath and U2, to name but three - but with Led Zeppelin the statistics speak for themselves. No other British band has sold as many records as Led Zeppelin over the years, and the numbers just keep on rising, in what has been one of the most remarkable music careers of all time. Led Zeppelin are an inspiration for as many bands today as they were back in the mid 1970s, which just goes to show that great music never goes out of fashion. The words have said all that they can, so for now revel in this DVD as a memento to one of the greatest global rock and roll bands of all time - Led Zeppelin...

LED ZEPPELIN
ALBUM BY ALBUM

Led Zeppelin – You either loved them or you hated them. In the seventies judging by the record sales and concert attendances the world over there were (and still are) a lot of people that loved them. To some they became the best rock band on the planet and they were certainly one of the most successful of all time. To others they were a prime target to ridicule and vilify.

No one however could deny the powerhouse of a rock band that they were, nor could anyone deny the consummate skill that these four dynamic musicians possessed. These four master musicians became rock gods in no uncertain terms. Listen, learn and read on…

LED ZEPPELIN

Atlantic 8216 Released 12th January 1969
Produced by Jimmy Page

Probably one of the best debut albums ever issued by a band. If there was ever an indication of how good a band Led Zeppelin were to become, then a good listen to this little gem was a sure fire way of becoming hooked. Ironically it was Led Zeppelin II that was to catapult the band to fame and fortune. Good as many of the tracks on Led Zeppelin II were, Led Zeppelin I was (and still is) a more cohesive and pleasurable album to listen to in one go.

The cover was very simple but incredibly effective and striking. See this one and its indelibly stamped in the memory. Classic start from a band that was to become one of the biggest bands in the classic rock era, if not the biggest.

GOOD TIMES BAD TIMES
(Page/Jones/Bonham)

This track was released as a single (Atlantic 2613) on 3/10/69 reaching number eighty in the US pop chart. As the opener of the debut it's a classic with its rather cool vocal and solid riff – certainly a good indicator of (some of) the things to come.

BABE I'M GONNA LEAVE YOU
(Bredon/Page/Plant)

With Robert Plant's haunting vocals this is certainly one of the high points on the album and quite possibly the bands career. Beautiful acoustic guitar playing with a subtle but literally smashing rhythm section creating wonderful interplay with Plant's vocal gymnastics, topped off with Jimmy Page's classy guitar breaks it didn't get much better than this as far as the mighty Zeppelin were concerned.

YOU SHOOK ME
(Dixon/Lenoir)

This is what early Led Zeppelin were masters at, heavy blues complemented by Plant's haunting vocals. Grungy slide guitar really sets this track in (slow) motion. This is probably the best rendition of Willie Dixon's classic track. John Paul Jones keyboard (probably a Hammond) really gives this track a period feel. Plant's harmonica just adds the spice to a classic feel.

DAZED AND CONFUSED
(Page)

Great guitar in this one, Dazed And Confused was a track Jimmy Page had penned before the formation of Led Zeppelin and he frequently played it with the last version of the Yardbirds. Not dissimilar from something Hendrix might have done several years earlier. This is classic Led Zeppelin and a song that was later extended live to over thirty minute epics with Jimmy Page cavorting with a cello bow. In the centre section the guitar is used to great effect even on the original studio version and for 1968 was obviously highly innovative. Thumping bass and extreme use of the c

YOUR TIME IS GONNA COME
(Page/Jones)

Segues from Dazed And Confused with a keyboard sound that although used sparingly by John Paul Jones was to become very much a Led Zeppelin sound. Nice gentle guitar from Jimmy gives this song a lovely feel. Along with Black Mountain side this track gives a nice respite from some rather exciting and heavy tracks now the album is on CD. In the days of vinyl of course this was a gentle (ish) start to side two.

BLACK MOUNTAIN SIDE
(Page)

One of many rather lovely instrumental acoustic pieces that Jimmy Page would add to the albums. This track was obviously an extension of White Summer which he had been playing in the Yardbirds. Interestingly White Summer was often played live by Jimmy Page in the early Led Zeppelin sets.

COMMUNICATION BREAKDOWN
(Page/Jones/Bonham)

Also released as the B-side to Good Times Bad Times which made a single that really had to be purchased if you like rockers! Classic frantic Zep song that became perfect for radio play. American radio loves it just as much today as in 1968!

I CAN'T QUIT YOU BABY
(Willie Dixon)

Another Willie Dixon classic that slows the pace down again. Although the song sounds rather dated today there is no doubting Jimmy Page's ability to take a classic like this and make it his own. With Robert Plant attacking the vocals it gave the song a whole new feel.

HOW MANY MORE TIMES
(Page/Jones/Bonham)

To many this minor epic was as good a song as Dazed And Confused. However it was never really performed and transformed into the live set in quite the same manner. The band certainly could have and should have! Great guitar work in this one with plenty of double tracking even at this early stage of the game. This track certainly displayed Jimmy Page's skill in the studio as well as a top guitar player. Brilliant all round playing from the band especially John Bonham. Great end to a classic debut album.

THE SINGLE

GOOD TIMES BAD TIMES
(Page/Jones/Bonham)

Released as a single (Atlantic 2613) on 3/10/69 reaching number eighty in the US pop chart. Backed with Communication Breakdown (Page/Jones/Bonham)

LED ZEPPELIN II

Atlantic 8236 Released October 22nd 1969
Produced by Jimmy Page

With a debut album that was as good as Led Zeppelin I it was always going to be a difficult task to keep the standard up. Material-wise they achieved this if not surpassed it with at least half of the tracks and the other half were certainly not bad. The tracks were obviously not honed as live numbers as much as most of its predecessor's material and as time has moved on one can really hear dynamic development of the studio tracks off Led Zeppelin II. Sometimes called 'The Brown Bomber' (One wonders whether this was because of the often 'muddy' sound!) Led Zeppelin II's greatest fault was the recording.

This was probably caused by several things: The album was recorded in a number of studios in different countries (seven in fact! And there were only nine songs), often while the band had heavy touring commitments. This gave the recordings a sonic inconsistency that had it been recorded today would probably not have posed such distinct differences because of digital recording techniques and facilities. Secondly, time has usually proven that a better album usually results from consistent and often intense recording periods. I.e. not hopping from studio to studio. Led Zeppelin I was certainly proof of how effective this could be, recorded in a matter of days on a relatively (for the day) tight budget the same results are rarely achieved when truck loads of money are poured into a project. Ironically it's the re-mastering of Led Zeppelin II that has really highlighted the studio inconsistencies as well. That aside no one can deny what a classic rock album it (very quickly) became or that it is indeed a great listen even today.

WHOLE LOTTA LOVE
(Page/Plant/Jones/Bonham)
Also released as a single (Atlantic 2690) on 11/7/69 reaching number four in the US pop charts. Certainly one of the classic rock songs of all time and although live brings out the best in the song the studio version was certainly not puss in boots. Great mdrumming and bass work from Bonham and Jones really pin the song down, the guitar work especially Jimmy's classic riff are certainly something to behold. Robert Plant's vocals were amongst the best efforts he ever committed to tape.

WHAT IS AND WHAT SHOULD NEVER BE
(Page/Plant)
A vastly under-rated track, this one really displayed how effective Led Zeppelin were at creating light and shade in their sound-scapes. Page's gentle slide guitar in this is a joy to hear as are his ballsy riffs. Best of all however is Plant's 'effected' vocals, that gave
the song (for its time) quite a futuristic feel. Classic use of early stereo phasing show mthat it's often the old and simple studio tricks that work best.

THE LEMON SONG
(Page/Plant/Jones/Bonham)
Although horrifically recorded (like quite a few numbers on this album) the song became a live favourite in the early days. Great (if a little dated) bass playing in this mone. The lyrical content of course was loved by all the young twenty something's and mteenagers in its heyday and one wonders whether it was this along with Plant's often sexual innuendo and antics that made this so popular because quite frankly it is not a brilliant song. Aptly named maybe.

THANK YOU
(Page/Plant)
Beautiful keyboard playing from John Paul Jones and wonderfully gentle guitar playing from Page gives this song a particularly pleasant intro. Again it's Robert Plant's 'effected' vocals that give this a sound that Led Zeppelin made their own.

Although not complex in composition, it maintains a rather clever feel throughout. It was a lovely end to the original side one of the vinyl, something that was ever so important before the continual play of CD's today.

HEARTBREAKER
(Page/Plant/Jones/Bonham)
To some this was the best song on the album. It certainly was the song with killer riff number two (or number one if you preferred it to Whole Lotta Love). As far as aclassic rock songgoes, it had everything. Great riffs throughout, fantastically vibrant solos, strong romping rhythm section and very cool vocals. Heartbreaker was a good song in 1969 and it's a good song today. Live, this was absolutely dynamite!

LIVING LOVING MAID (SHE'S JUST A WOMAN)
(Page/Plant)
Also released as the B-side to Whole Lotta Love. Not a bad little number for a rock and roller and it was a sensible choice for a B-side. This one was always going to be pleasant album filler.

RAMBLE ON
(Page/Plant)
Showing the gentle side of Zeppelin at the beginning, the song soon progresses with a nice grungy riff before returning to a gentle section again with rather wonderful harmonic guitar solo from Jimmy Page. Classic early Zeppelin.

MOBY DICK
(Page/Jones/Bonham)

Another killer riff from Jimmy Page and the band are off on this intrepid vehicle, which became the platform for John Bonham to really show off his wares. Live, this track became a mainstay and no one can deny how classy Bonham was when he really set to it with this one in an arena. This original studio version was always going to be hard to make work because drum solos really do not work for anyone (except possibly other drummers!) unless they are in a vibrant live environment. The band did however need a 'show-off' song for Bonham and this is exactly what this was.

BRING IT ON HOME
(Page/Plant)

Absolutely stunning blues track from Jimmy and the Boys. With a simple but wonderfully sonic bass start, great harmonica and Plant's haunting vocals the track rips into another one of Page's magic riffs. Riffing like this is something Led Zeppelin were particularly good at and this tune is a perfect example of just how good the ycould be. Great way to finish the album.

THE SINGLE

WHOLE LOTTA LOVE
(Page/Plant/Jones/Bonham)

(Atlantic 2690) on 11/7/69 reaching number four in the US pop charts. Backed with Living Loving Maid (She's Just A Woman) (Page/Plant).

LED ZEPPELIN III

Atlantic 7201 Released on October 5th 1970
Produced by Jimmy Page.

This was the critical third album. Did it work? Well yes and no is the answer. The album is a minor triumph and certainly an improvement on the previous mtwo efforts by the band, especially in recording terms. The sales however were not what some might call record breaking compared to Led Zeppelin II. It has however become a favourite with fans over the years.

It certainly remains the easiest and most enjoyable of the early albums to listen to in one go. Recording was also a lot more cohesive, organised and relaxed than the previous efforts for Led Zeppelin II.

The band decamped to the now famous Headley Grange in Hampshire with the Rolling Stones Mobile in tow. A wealth of material was laid down, some later even appearing on the Physical Graffiti double set. Several numbers were recorded in Olympic Studio's and Island Studios in London. The album retains a far more balanced feel than Led Zeppelin II however and this is almost certainly due to it being recorded (and mostly mixed) in the UK during a period where the band had allowed themselves to unwind for a while.

IMMIGRANT SONG
(Page/Plant)

One of the most identifiable songs Led Zeppelin ever recorded. With Robert Plant's haunting vocal, driving guitar, bass and drums, this was a song that no one could ignore. With it's Nordic/Celtic lyrics and general feel it is a song one wants to play mover and over again. It could also have been an interesting number had they chosen to really stretch it out in the live environment. Released as a single (Atlantic 2777) on the 11/5/70 it reached number sixteen in the US pop chart. Backed with a non-LP track entitled Hey, Hey, What Can I Do? the single became extremely collectable.

FRIENDS
(Page/Plant)

With off key guitar and whining vocals and one might be forgiven for thinking this track might never work. But work it does and extremely well, especially as a very clever connector piece of music between the thumping Immigrant Song and the catchy and clever Celebration Day. Use of the mellotron and moog gives this song a haunting feel.

CELEBRATION DAY
(Page/Plant/Jones)

This original studio version is an early Zeppelin mini-classic and one that became a favourite in the live shows. With its clever hooks and Plant's haunting and vibrant vocals, this really makes the song shine.

SINCE I'VE BEEN LOVING YOU
(Page/Plant/Jones)

Certainly one of the best blues numbers ever penned and played by Led Zeppelin. It was this type of number (and this song in particular) that Led Zeppelin were absolute mmasters at. No one to date has ever really bettered the mixtures of blues and rock in the way it is captured by Led Zeppelin, certainly in the top five songs Led Zeppelin ever issued. The official live versions are brilliant as well (the first making an appearance on the film version of The Song Remains The Same). Several versions that have been made available via bootlegs are nothing short of stunning. Since I've Been Loving You contains some of the best playing ever recorded by Jimmy Page. A blues guitarists dream!

OUT ON THE TILES
(Page/Plant/Bonham)

End song on the original side one of the vinyl. What a way to end a side it was too! Heavy, ballsy rocker that when you hear this one finish it leaves you gagging for more.

GALLOWS POLE
(Traditional. Arranged by Jimmy Page/Robert Plant)

Opening track on side two of the original vinyl Gallows Pole wasn't actually penned by Led Zeppelin but was rather an interpretation of an older number and it was one mof the best 'covers' ever attempted by Led Zeppelin.

TANGERINE
(Jimmy Page)

Another very cool semi-acoustic number, this time penned solely by Jimmy Page. Robert Plant's vocals once again work ever so well as does John Paul Jones use of various keyboard toys. Cool link number and a perfect addition to a near perfect album.

THAT'S THE WAY
(Page/Plant)

Lovely acoustic number with relatively tranquil vocals from Robert Plant. When Led Zeppelin tried their hand at these acoustic numbers it was often hit or miss. This one certainly worked very very well. Very cool lyrics as well. Nice.

BRON-Y-AUR STOMP
(Page/Plant/Jones)

Another acoustic number that the band blended into a stomp. It's kind of quaint and does actually work even if it does go on a little too long. Robert Plant's vocals (like so much of his singing on this album) are rather cool. Influenced, according to the band by a small derelict cottage in Snowdonia.

HATS OFF TO (ROY) HARPER

(Traditional. Arranged by Charles Obscure)

Every album has to have a weird number and this is it! Very cool guitar from Jimmy Page and some of the weirdest vocals from Robert Plant. Old fashioned use of separate left and right channel use for vocals and guitar. This track was as near as filler that the band ever got to on this release. It's not a bad number all in all but the album really could have done with a nice heavy number (or two) to finish with.

THE SINGLE

IMMIGRANT SONG

(Page/Plant)

Released as a single (Atlantic 2777) on the 11/5/70 it reached number sixteen in the US pop chart. It was backed with Hey, Hey, What Can I Do (Page/Plant/Jones/Bonham) – recorded in 1970 at Island Studios, London.

> "You might have heard that I played on a Burt Bacharach record. It's true. I never knew what I was doing "
>
> Jimmy Page

LED ZEPPELIN IV

Atlantic 7208 Released November 8th 1971
Produced by Jimmy Page

Certainly the album that put Led Zeppelin very near the top, if not the top of the rock mountain! To record this album the band once again decamped to the depths of the Hampshire countryside and set-up (recording) shop at Headley Grange with the Rolling Stones Mobile unit. Led Zeppelin IV was to quickly become known in the industry as a Monster. It literally sold by the truckload all over America and indeed in most other territories the band already had penetration into, which quite frankly was most of the western world.

BLACK DOG

(Page/Plant/Jones)

One of the most identifiable numbers in rock music let alone Led Zeppelin's cannon and written about a dog that died in one of the rooms at Headley Grange. The dog was black of course! Black Dog was the perfect opener to what would become for many the perfect Led Zeppelin album. Certainly it was a continuation in feel and style from Immigrant Song from Led Zeppelin III. Classic heavy Led Zeppelin at their best. Also released as a single (Atlantic 2849) on the 2nd December 1971 reaching number 15 in the US charts. Every hard rock compilation known to man should include this one!

ROCK AND ROLL

(Page/Plant/Jones/Bonham)

Released as a single (Atlantic 2865) on 21st February 1972 and reached number 47 in he US pop chart. A show opener for many a year this straightforward rocker is yet another track that has become so identifiable for the band. Even the guitar solos work well and John Paul Jones' classic rock and roll piano tops it all off perfectly. Another Zep classic.

THE BATTLE OF EVERMORE
(Page/Plant)

When Led Zeppelin decided to go the acoustic route there were very few artists that could compete with them and The Battle Of Evermore was a perfect example of just how good they could be. One of the best acoustic numbers from Zeppelin, this number has also become famous for the vocal contributions from Sandy Denny. Page's guitar, Plant's and Denny's haunting vocals create a dramatic and mystical feel throughout. Live, this track when delivered properly, was an absolute beauty.

STAIRWAY TO HEAVEN
(Page/Plant)

Along with Four Sticks this was one of two tracks from this album to be recorded at Island Studios in London. A beautiful epic of a song, this was to go on to become one of the most identifiable and long lasting songs in the history of Rock and Roll. Everything in this recording was perfect. Jimmy Page's lilting acoustic guitar that later he changes to (often a double necked) electric guitar where he displays a hell hath no fury guitar epic. Robert Plant's rather mystical and poetic lyric is delivered to perfection from beginning to end. Bonham's drums which enter a little over four minutes into the song and John Paul Jones bass playing really get this song underway in no uncertain terms. With Page's amazingly simple (sounding) solos and Robert mPlant's upbeat delivery for the latter part of the song, this was destined to become an air guitar epic.

Interestingly it appears the inspiration for much of the guitar-based hooks were borrowed (without much, if any acknowledgement as it happens) from the class American act Spirit and their song entitled Taurus from their debut album. Taurus was written by the hugely under-rated guitar player Randy California and then recorded by Spirit in 1967 nearly four years before Stairway to Heaven was penned and recorded. Interestingly Led Zeppelin had also been on tour with Spirit in the US several years prior to the recording on Led Zeppelin IV. It has always seemed a shame that Randy California never appeared to get credit for his rather major inspiration and contribution to Rock. Led Zeppelin, good as they were, were certainly not adverse to 'borrowing' (often with out crediting) other peoples songs and making them their own. Stairway, of course, has become the classic of Zeppelin classics and quite possibly the most popular rock song of all time.

MISTY MOUNTAIN HOP
(Page/Plant/Jones)

Also used as the B-side to the Black Dog single. Misty Mountain Romp is what this mone should have been called. Classic multi-tracked vocals give this number an unusual (for Zeppelin) feel. Plant's vocals are outstanding in this tune, which once you got used to really grow on you.

FOUR STICKS
(Page/Plant)

WHEN THE LEVEE BREAKS

(Page/Plant/Jones/John Bonham/Memphis Minnie)

Well we all know an epic when we hear one and this track is certainly that. Not a song that was (or is) easily accessible at first. However once this gets going and you have played it several times (preferably repeatedly) it will really grow on you. There is great harmonica playing on this one and a wonderful lilting guitar riff from Jimmy Page. Robert Plant's haunting vocals really suck the listener in during the seven plus minutes the song lasts for and the rhythm section and cleverly repetitive riff will just blow you away if this is played (very) loud. Great end to a classic album.

THE SINGLES

BLACK DOG

(Page/Plant/Jones)

Released as a single (Atlantic 2849) on the 2nd December 1971 reaching number 15 in the US charts. Backed with Misty Mountain Hop (Page/Plant/Jones).

ROCK AND ROLL

(Page/Plant/Jones/Bonham)

Released as a single (Atlantic 2865) on 21st February 1972 and reached number 47 in the US pop chart. Backed with Four Sticks (Page/Plant).

HOUSES OF THE HOLY

Atlantic 7255 Released March 28th 1973
Produced by Jimmy Page

After the release and immense success of Led Zeppelin IV the fifth studio effort was always going to be a hard act to follow. The easy way might have been to close the period off with a cracking live album. The band as we now know certainly had a wealth of live material to work with had they chosen to do so. Instead they hired Stargroves, deep in rural England and called in the Rolling Stones Mobile recording unit once again. Six of the eight tracks to grace the album were recorded there with one being laid down at Island Studio's in London, one track even being recorded in their old haunt at Headley Grange. All tracks were engineered by Eddie Kramer using the Rolling Stones Mobile. Interestingly the album was mixed by three separate (and quite different) engineers; Eddie Kramer mixed five tracks at Electric Ladyland Studios in New York, Keith Harwood worked his magic at Olympic Studios in London and Andy Johns also mixed No Quarter at Olympic. Considering the different people involved the album has remained a cohesive piece of work. Certainly not the bands best (although the sales were monstrous) nonetheless the album is a milestone in Zeppelin's history.

THE SONG REMAINS THE SAME

(Page/Plant)

Good ballsy start to the fifth studio effort. The Song Remains The Same became a stage favourite with both band and fans for many a year after its release. It was mapparent from the first passages of this song that Led Zeppelin had entered a more msophisticated level of song writing and recording even though this song basically utilized drums, bass and guitar along with Robert Plant's rousing vocals.

THE RAIN SONG
(Page/Plant)

One of the most beautiful songs ever recorded by Led Zeppelin and one that contains wonderful mellotron playing by John Paul Jones. Segueing from The Song Remains The Same this number was hugely popular live. All in all top class.

OVER THE HILLS AND FAR AWAY
(Page/Plant)

Released as a single (Atlantic 2970) on the 24th of May 1973 and reached number 51 in the US pop chart. Led Zeppelin had really broken away from their earlier style with most of Houses Of The Holy, however Over The Hills And Far Away was a little glimpse in some ways at the past. Classic Zep riff with Robert Plant's distinctive vocal it was interspaced with rather wonderful acoustic overtones. Top this with a clever guitar solo and it was obvious this should be released as a single.

THE CRUNGE
(Bonham/Jones/Page/Plant)

Released as the B-side to the D'yer Mak'er single. The single should have been the only place the track was ever made available as it is a serious contender for the 'biggest mpiece of crap, Ever!' prize. There really is not a redeeming feature to this song apart from the musicianship, which as usual is faultless and maybe the exception being John Paul Jones dabble with a synthesiser. Why the band ever recorded something like this is anyone's guess. Still it was the seventies. Today one can easily programme it straight out of the CD play-list or better still delete it from the ipod. Forever.

DANCING DAYS
(Page/Plant)

Released as the B-side to Over The Hills And Far Away. With a song as good as this as a B-side, fans were really being treated to a double A-side and in fact in a number of countries it was this B-side that was plugged by the radio. Very cool slide playing from Jimmy Page and subtle use of organ by John Paul Jones. This was also one of the first songs composed by Page and Plant that had Middle Eastern influences within, a theme both artists were to revisit with vigour in later years.

D'YER MAK'ER
(Page/Plant/Jones/Bonham)

Released as a single (Atlantic 2986) on the 17th of September 1973 and reached number 20 in the US pop chart. Another very cool single and a song that was a far cry mfrom the earlier Led Zeppelin sound. This was certainly a very cool song to try and sing in a bar under the influence, if you could remember the words. Excellent offbeat drumming from John Bonham.

NO QUARTER
(Page/Plant/Jones)

Quite possibly the best track to feature the many talents of John Paul Jones. His instrumentation contribution comprised of rather wonderful and haunting Synthesiser piano, grand piano and synthesised bass. Live it was an epic. Robert Plant's treated vocals are haunting and certainly contribute an immense amount to mthe feel of the song.

THE OCEAN
(Page/Plant/Jones/Bonham)

Not the best track ever recorded by the band but a more than suitable album filler. All band members aside from John Bonham contributed do-wop backing vocals. Interestingly the song comes into its own in a live environment as proven in the version released on How The West Was Won.

THE SINGLES

OVER THE HILLS AND FAR AWAY
(Page/Plant)

Released as a single (Atlantic 2970) on the 24th of May 1973 and reached number 51 in the US pop chart. Backed with Dancing Days (Page/Plant).

D'YER MAK'ER
(Page/Plant/Jones/Bonham)

Released as a single (Atlantic 2986) on the 17th of September 1973 and reached number 20 in the US pop chart. Backed with The Crunge (Bonham/Jones/Page/Plant).

> " I left session work to join the Yardbirds, at a third of the bread, because I wanted to play again "

Jimmy Page

PHYSICAL GRAFFITI

Swan Song 2-200 Released February 24th 1975
Produced by Jimmy Page

Certainly the best post Stairway to Heaven album Physical Graffiti was a double masterpiece delivered in an innovative sleeve design. Quite frankly there are few covers from the seventies that had the impact this one did. One has to say this applies to the original vinyl version. CD size just doesn't work! Spread over two long players the songs and the delivery were mostly nothing short of stunning. The band once again went camping in Hampshire at Headley Grange, this time with Ronnie Lane's Mobile in tow. Eight tracks that were laid down in 1974 eventually graced the album; the remainder were recorded between 1970 and 1972. Two from the 1972 Stargroves sessions for Houses Of The Holy, two more from the 1971 sessions at Headley Grange, one each from 1970 (Island Studios), 1971 (Island Studios) and 1972 (Olympic Studios).

Totalling fifteen tracks the album was a bumper box full of goodies. Physical Graffiti is undoubtedly one of the best double studio sets ever issued by a rock and roll band. As an aside: There are several bootlegs floating around with out-takes and alternate versions of much of the 1974 Headley Grange sessions. Needless to say these make for absolutely fascinating listening for fans of Physical Graffiti and for live versions one need look no further than the infamous Earls Court live recordings.

CUSTARD PIE
(Page/Plant)

Recorded at Headley Grange in 1974 with Ronnie Lanes Mobile and completed at Olympic Studio's, London. Listen to this track and then to Trampled Under Foot and one must wonder if they were recorded on the same day! Custard Pie was however a promising start to a long awaited album. An album that did virtually nothing to disappoint from start to finish.

THE ROVER
(Page/Plant)

Recorded at Stargroves, England in 1972 using the Rolling Stones Mobile and finished off at Olympic Studios, London. One of the best hard groove tracks ever recorded by Led Zeppelin. Star delivery by all members of what was so obviously by now, a band that gelled perfectly. Exceptional playing by Jimmy Page. An edited version of this track may well have made a great rock single.

IN MY TIME OF DYING
(Page/Plant/Jones/Bonham)

Recorded at Headley Grange in 1974 with Ronnie Lanes Mobile the track contains over eleven minutes of mind-blowing playing and brilliance from all concerned. Jimmy Page's guitar rarely got much better than what was contained in the grooves of this track. It certainly contains some of the best heavy slide playing Page ever committed to tape.

HOUSES OF THE HOLY
(Page/Plant)

Recorded in 1972 at Olympic Studios in London the title track for Houses Of The Holy never actually made the album it was supposed to grace. This was a little strange really as it was actually far better than a number of other cuts that were included on the Houses Of The Holy release. Subtle but cool guitar by Jimmy Page, especially at the end of the song.

TRAMPLED UNDER FOOT
(Page/Plant/Jones)

Recorded at Headley Grange in 1974 and completed at Olympic Studios in London, this track was also released as a single (Swan Song 70102) on the 4/2/75 and reached number 38 in the US pop charts. A clever funky romp that featured some fine electric piano playing. Trampled Under Foot featured fantastic guitar throughout and the rest of the band really delivered the goods with this one even if it was an unusual choice for a single. Robert Plant's vocals were in fine form and he rarely got better as a cut and thrust singer as he did in this one.

KASHMIR
(Page/Plant/Bonham)

Recorded at Headley Grange in 1974 with Ronnie Lanes Mobile Studio and completed at Olympic Studios in London. With faint eastern and Arabic influences this was the track that in turn influenced a lot of future material recorded by both Robert Plant and Jimmy Page. Kashmir has become a Led Zeppelin classic in no uncertain terms. Play this with the volume knob cranked at around about full and you will easily be able to tell why. The rhythm section is spot on and Page's guitar cannot be faulted. Robert Plant's vocals are once again top notch.

IN THE LIGHT
(Page/Plant/Jones)

Recorded at Headley Grange in 1974 with Ronnie Lanes Mobile and completed at Olympic Studio's, London. With an intriguing keyboard intro by John Paul Jones lasting for over one and a half minutes the second disc in the original vinyl was already off in an interesting direction. Where side one and two of the original vinyl really sounded like a cohesive album, side three and four was a varied collection of tracks. Weirdly it all worked very well. Great playing by all concerned.

BRON-YR-AUR
(Page)

Recorded in 1970 at Island Studios, London. One of Jimmy Page's masterful acoustic ditties. Brilliant in its sonic delivery and simplicity. Interestingly recorded around the time of Led Zeppelin III where the acoustic influences were at their highest for the guitar player.

DOWN BY THE SEASIDE
(Page/Plant)

Recorded in 1971 at Island Studios, London. One of the best (soft) vocal deliveries from Robert Plant. The track also featured a wonderful backing vocal sound, subtle but classy keyboards and when the song reaches midpoint it grooves on wonderfully before returning to that ever so English sound encapsulated from the beginning of the song.

TEN YEARS GONE
(Page/Plant)

Recorded at Headley Grange in 1974 with Ronnie Lanes Mobile and completed at Olympic Studio's, London. After Down By The Seaside and just when you thought the music couldn't be bettered appeared this little (six and a half minute) number.

Amongst the best tracks ever recorded by Led Zeppelin it had a beautiful mixture of gentle and heavy all in the same track. The playing of Jones and Bonham keeping it all together with Jimmy Page's jaw dropping playing delivering the goods to wondrous effect. Once again Robert Plant delivered absolutely stunning singing at all stages of the game. Beautiful and immensely powerful song.

NIGHT FLIGHT
(John Paul Jones/Jimmy Page/Robert Plant)

Recorded at Headley Grange in 1971 with the Rolling Stones mobile and completed at Island Studios, London.

Good gentle rocker delivered with superb drumming from Bonham. John Paul Jones keyboards really give the song a gentle but full sound while Jimmy Page handles the riffs and solo's perfectly as usual. This would probably have made a sensible second single had they chosen to release one.

THE WANTON SONG
(Page/Plant)

Recorded at Headley Grange in 1974 with Ronnie Lanes Mobile and completed at Olympic Studio's, London. Although not a particularly memorable track it's certainly better than just album filler. Good riffs and a nice listen but at the same time it's not one you will be humming for days. Plant's vocals are certainly of the type that must have influenced David Coverdale in later years when he teamed up with Jimmy Page in the early 1990's.

BOOGIE WITH STU
(Page/Plant/Jones/Bonham)

Recorded at Headley Grange in 1971 with the Rolling Stones mobile. Great little rock and roll (slow) boogie. The band were obviously having fun and although it was an older hitherto unreleased track it worked surprisingly well.

BLACK COUNTRY WOMAN
(Page/Plant)

Recorded at Stargroves in 1972 with the Rolling Stones Mobile. Another nice gentle acoustic number that was far more than casual album filler. Robert Plant's vocals are as emotional as ever and even though this was recorded two years prior to the 1974 Headley Grange sessions it actually fits in quite well. Some wonderful harmonica graces the grooves from time to time.

SICK AGAIN **(Page/Plant)**

Recorded at Headley Grange in 1974 with Ronnie Lanes Mobile and completed at Olympic Studio's, London. Back to

the rock for the exit song. Classic mid period Zeppelin with a great riff. The band is in full swing with this one, especially Robert Plant. The song is reminiscent of material that ended up on Houses Of The Holy. It's hard for any band to hold the listeners attention over a double album. Led Zeppelin in the main achieved that with this classic double set.

THE SINGLE

TRAMPLED UNDER FOOT
(Page/Plant/Jones)
Released as a single (Swan Song 70102) on the 4/2/75 and reached number 38 in the US pop charts. Backed with Black Country Woman (Page/Plant).

> "Organ was in fact, was always my first love, but for session playing I found it much easier to carry a base guitar to work than a Hammond organ"

John Paul Jones

THE SONG REMAINS THE SAME
Swan Song SS 2-201 Released 1976.
Produced by Jimmy Page.

Classic film soundtrack from the long awaited film. Interestingly the LP and film version did differ substantially as far as content was concerned. The delivery however did not, this was as classy as Led Zeppelin always were live. Recorded live at Madison Square Gardens, New York in 1973.

ROCK AND ROLL
(Page/Plant/Jones/Bonham)
The show opener for many a day after its debut this is a classic live interpretation of a classic rock 'n' roll song. No–one could ever complain about the delivery on this one!

CELEBRATION DAY
(Page/Plant/Jones)
A vastly under-rated song from Led Zeppelin III the live version captured the magic even better. Simple but effective guitar solo's from Jimmy Page. Robert Plant's vocals were perfect for getting the concertgoers boogieing at this point. Not included on the original film version.

THE SONG REMAINS THE SAME
(Page/Plant)
From their most recent studio offering at the time these Madison Square Garden concerts were filmed the band really keep up the pace with this one. Interestingly this song, although the live delivery was very good (as were most songs Led Zeppelin performed live) was not really a lot different from the original studio version. The studio version was a strong song with strong delivery in the first place. Like the studio version this live number segues perfectly into The Rain Song.

THE RAIN SONG
(Page/Plant)

This was the last song on the original side one of the double vinyl release. What a beautiful song this was in its original studio version. Here, in it's live context it becomes quite magical. Maybe its Plant's vocals or maybe its just the audience appreciation as the song commences, whatever it is it always seemed to work ever so well live. Watch the film stoned when this is playing and all might be revealed, its just one of those numbers.

DAZED AND CONFUSED
(Jimmy Page)

This is what Led Zeppelin were all about! Live, epic numbers where virtuoso performances could be taken to the limit. The song live was a perfect example of all of the above with more than a little show-off factor thrown in. After Jimmy Page's cello bow antics, his perfectly executed guitar work and Robert Plant's haunting vocals one was certainly left dazed and confused. The original studio version was a little under six and a half minutes and in the early days the band could stretch it to ten minutes or so. Soon after it was reaching eighteen plus minutes and by 1973 it was reaching twenty-seven minutes, sometimes longer! This was definitely a song that encouraged a certain amount of substance abuse in the seventies! Dynamic and exciting playing from every band member made this a showcase piece for years. Today it still retains the vibrancy and excitement.

NO QUARTER
(Page/Plant/Jones)

Another track from Houses Of The Holy, this one was really supposed to be the showcase of John Paul Jones' keyboard playing including keyboard bass. It certainly displayed his virtuosity and it also contained classic passages of John Bonham's dynamic drumming, sparse but very clever use of Page's guitar and of course fantastic vocal from Robert Plant. The audiovisual experience of the film version is fantastic if you are in the correct frame of mind.

STAIRWAY TO HEAVEN
(Page/Plant)

Certainly one of the most important, most loved and certainly most played (especially on American Radio!) songs of all time. Live, the track comes to life in a way studio recordings do not often achieve. Although not the best live version ever heard (several well known bootlegs contain absolutely dynamite versions) this version nonetheless is a joy to listen to.

MOBY DICK
(Page/Jones/Bonham)

Always a bit of a dubious offering as a studio track Moby Dick really came into its own when (literally) hammered out live. This was the track that showcased John Bonham's immense drum and percussion talent and his brute strength and stamina. Rarely, with the exception of Cozy Powell has there been a drummer who could hit the skins with so much skill as John Bonham. He may not have been the most intricate of drummers but he could surely deliver the goods in no uncertain terms, with or without drumsticks. With a musical introduction consisting of a classic Page riff lasting for a little over a minute the rest of the band were able to retire offstage for ten minutes or so. With the stories that abound as to what various members got up to offstage (or under the stage) while Bonham was doing his thing its little wonder the rest of the band were keen to keep a long drum solo in their set! Still that's rock and roll! The best way to listen to this track however is while watching the filmed version on a very big screen.

WHOLE LOTTA LOVE
(Page/Plant/Jones/Bonham)

This version was recorded live some four years afters its release on Led Zeppelin II and it really is a joy to listen to, very loud! Containing parts of numerous rock, boogie and blues covers and even segments of other Zep songs this version of Whole Lotta Love is better listened to while staring at the big screen version from the film, that way you really get the seeing is believing feeling that this band were nearly always able to achieve live. Classic

Zeppelin delivered live. What else could you want?

PRESENCE

Swan Song 8416 Released March 31st 1976
Produced by Jimmy Page

Recorded and mixed at the famous Musicland Studios in Munich, Germany during November and December 1975. The album sported a rather interesting and clever cover featuring obelisks designed by Hipgnosis. Someone had fun at the photo shoots all at Zeppelin's expense in more ways than one that's for sure! Weird album cover or not, this was the long awaited album and to the Zeppelin starved masses in the seventies it by and large delivered the goods. Sure it was not Physical Graffiti but it was a very good album with some exceptional tracks held within the grooves. When the songs were good they were very very good but when they were bad they were awful. The cracks from a raucous rock and roll style were certainly starting to show.

ACHILLES LAST STAND

(Page/Plant)

At nearly ten and a half minutes Achilles was a real return to a classic Zeppelin epic. With a rolling romp of a start and brilliant drumming from John Bonham this was a more than healthy start for a long awaited album. The many guitar tracks comprised a subtle heaviness throughout the song that was cleverly held together by Robert Plant's almost off-world vocals. Even the solo's really followed the flow of the song and at times were the perfect foil for Bonham's machine gun attacks on the toms. In fact there are parts of Achilles Last Stand that do contain remnants of Hendrix's Machine Gun from the Band Of Gypsy's period. This is a wonderful song that in 1976 proved to be a great start to an album many had waited for gleefully for several years.

FOR YOUR LIFE

(Page/Plant)

A track that could quite easily have come from the Physical Graffiti sessions. Although not outstanding it does have its moments and for most fans would certainly grow on them. John Bonham's drumming and Jimmy Page's guitar are quite something but the track does take some patience and careful listening before it slowly hooks you.

ROYAL ORLEANS

(Bonham/Jones/Page/Plant)

Released as the B-side to Candy Store Rock (Swan Song 70110). If this track was anything was to go by it would bring down in flames the accolades for the debut track! Although not Zeppelins worst track it was not far off it! Why Zeppelin ever bothered with the rubbishy little rock and roll ditties I will never know. However one only has to listen to Robert Plant's work with The Honey Drippers and some of the rather more boring solo tracks to know where the major influence for this may have come from. The playing was superb but as they say, good material shines. This didn't in 1976 and it doesn't now. Calling it filler is being polite. It would have been perfect if this had only ever appeared as a B-side and something much more appropriate had graced its place on the album.

NOBODY'S FAULT BUT MINE

(Page/Plant)

The opener for the original side two of the vinyl, the band more than redeemed themselves with this one. This is absolutely classic hard rock Zep! Had this been released as a single with massive promotion it could well have blown most of the crappy punk material that was starting to appear well into the weeds. The song is well written and extremely well played and is certainly a song that should only be played at a level your neighbours can hear. Five blocks away! If any song on this album displayed Bonham's talent as one of the best hard rock drummers around at the time then this is it. Sure there were (and still are) far more skilful drummers around but he certainly had a 'feel'. This song displayed that feel perfectly. Robert Plant's vocals are classic Zep in this one as well. Shame he doesn't play stuff like this today.

CANDY STORE ROCK
(Page/Plant)

Released as the albums first single (Swan Song 70110) on the 18th June 1976. Although this was never likely to become a classic Led Zeppelin number it was a rather interesting attempt at something Elvis might have attempted had he been in the band. Reasonably good guitar solo's pop up here and there however. Enough said really.

HOTS ON FOR NOWHERE
(Page/Plant)

Maybe the band had the philosophy that as long as they did one or two blinding tracks then they could get away with padding an album with some rubbishy numbers. If they did then this song was certainly good examples of this. The song really doesn't go anywhere and quite frankly has to be classed as one of the more boring attempts at rock and roll by a band that had made quite a name for themselves with a track entitled, well, Rock And Roll. Fantastic as much of the Zeppelin cannon is, there is also plenty of throw away material. Should someone ever put a compilation together of Zeppelin tracks ones would rather not hear then this is a very good contender for number one. Aptly titled really. Not far off utter crap and just when you think the ending has arrived they add more for torture.

TEA FOR ONE
(Page/Plant)

Just when you thought all was lost, out of the hat comes this little white rabbit! This is probably one of the best blues numbers ever attempted by the mighty Led Zeppelin. Anyone who loves the blues would be unlikely to ever get sick of hearing this one. This is classic Led Zeppelin blues and when you hear this, one wonders why the album needed to have some of the other rubbishy little numbers included. Another of these or even extend it to double its length and most fans would have been in blues heaven.

Certainly reminiscent of Since I've Been Loving You from Led Zeppelin III it really does take on a feel of its own. This was a real stretch back to the bands early influences and early days and the song has brilliant performances by all concerned. What a way to finish an album! Now, in the days of CD's or I-pod's we can all program the throwaway tracks and just play the four high quality numbers that grace this album. This was certainly the hidden jewel in the crown as far as Presence was concerned. Simple, effective, bone-crunching blues that can make you feel like your soul is being ripped from your body. Not many blues players can achieve that to the level Page did with this one. Classic, classy stuff!

THE SINGLE

CANDY STORE ROCK
(Page/Plant)

Released as the albums first single (Swan Song 70110) on the 18th June 1976. Backed with Royal Orleans (Bonham/Jones/Page/Plant) – this was probably the worst single ever released by the band.

IN THROUGH THE OUT DOOR

Swan Song 16002 Released August 15th
1979 Produced by Jimmy Page

Recorded in late 1978 at Abba's Polar Studio's in
Stockholm, Sweden the album was mixed back in the UK.
Certainly an under-rated album and one that largely gets
forgotten in the greater scheme of things. It did however
suffer from the same basic problem that Presence did in
that when the material was good it was very very good
but when it was bad it was awful! The album contained a
number of songs that had Led Zeppelin remained a major
touring entity then the good numbers would have no doubt
shone. However with John Bonham's untimely death these
were by and large lost with the tragic chain of events and of
course by the complete shutdown of touring and break-up
of the band.

The albums cover was an interesting affair as well having
several different versions of the cover. The more cynical
might say that the album sales went as well as they did due
to the fact that fans had to collect multiple copies! I don't
think so!

IN THE EVENING
(Page/Plant/Jones)

One thing Led Zeppelin were VERY good at was choosing a
bone crunching and memorable track as an opener. In The
Evening certainly maintained the tradition in that respect.
The album has a great feel to it right from the start and
contains some of the best 'heavy' solo's from Jimmy Page
in many a year. With beautiful semi acoustic passages in
there and a highly memorable riff this song was a guitar
players dream. Plant's desperate vocals really top it all off.
Classic Zeppelin and a great start to an album. This should
have been the single to kick off the album.

SOUTH BOUND SAUREZ
(Jones/Plant)

Although not as bad as some of the throwaway numbers on Presence this is not exactly what one would call classic classy Led Zeppelin. It's well played and no doubt they had fun playing it but it does show that they may well have been struggling for decent material. There is a good guitar solo in the middle, which redeems the song a little. Not by much however.

FOOL IN THE RAIN
(Page/Plant/Jones)

Released as a single (Swan Song 71003) on 12/7/79, this reached number 21 in the US pop chart. Not a bad track but neither is it a brilliant attempt either. It was certainly not the best choice for a single by a band like Led Zeppelin. At best this is good album material although John Paul Jones piano playing and John Bonham's drumming is quite something to listen to. Simple but effective.

HOT DOG
(Page/Plant)

Released as the B-side of the Fool In The Rain single and a B-side is all it should have ever been! Another of those rather sad fillers. Interestingly there has never been an album put together (yet) of all these throwaway numbers. My guess is that if there ever was it would not sell in great numbers! Great playing however and once again John Paul Jones shines in this one. At least Elvis had been several years gone by this stage. Rock God Robert Plant may have been, Elvis he was not. There was only ever one Elvis.

CAROUSELAMBRA
(Page/Plant/Jones)

The lost epic? Well maybe not, however the song really does start to deliver some classic Zeppelin to the listener's ears. Carouselambra contained vibrant and heavy use of keyboards and this really added to the song in no uncertain terms. Robert Plant's vocal lilt added to this number perfectly. He always had a clever way of laying down a rather haunting feel to many of the Zeppelin epics and this song was no exception.

Although Jimmy Page's guitar playing was not as prominent in this as in past epics, however when he lets loose it really works. It's a shame the band didn't really get a chance to extend this track live as it would have been a perfect vehicle for Page and Plant to exercise some of their classic live interplay of former years. Actually the track is mildly reminiscent of some of the sound-scapes delivered on the Houses Of The Holy album six years earlier.

ALL MY LOVE
(Plant/Jones)

Very un-Zeppelin like this track was but it worked very well. Very clever use of mellotron from John Paul Jones and wonderful vocals from Robert Plant this was clearly a song that Jimmy Page just played along to. Beautifully. His guitar sound and textures really create a relaxed but rather tragic feel to the song. The weird (for Led Zeppelin) keyboard use also added to the song in no uncertain terms. All this was under-pinned by a strong but subtle riff. Interestingly when one listens to Robert Plant's second solo album Principle Of Moments one cannot help but draw some comparisons. Had Led Zeppelin stayed together there would almost certainly have mbeen a few more numbers like this. Nice song.

I'M GONNA CRAWL
(Page/Plant/Jones)

After All My Love one might have expected a bone-cruncher of a song to finish the malbum. Not this time however, and oh how it works. This song really made the album. mPlant's vocals were nothing short of brilliant in capturing and maintaining a feel of tragedy and desperation and how poetic was that to be within a matter of months Jimmy Page's guitar playing once again captured the moment beautifully and John Paul Jones and John Bonham created a wonderful ambience to one of the best 'quieter' songs Zeppelin attempted in their later year. Certainly not a disgraceful Swan Song even if that was unintentional.

THE SINGLE

FOOL IN THE RAIN
(Page/Plant/Jones)
Released as a single (Swan Song 71003) on 12/7/79, this reached number 21 in the US pop chart. Backed with Hot Dog (Page/Plant)

CODA

Swan Song 90051 Released November 20th 1982
Produced by Jimmy Page

Released post John Bonham's death and of course after Page, Plant and Jones had effectively disbanded Led Zeppelin, Coda is a surprisingly balanced album to listen to when one considers it was a collection of hitherto unreleased material recorded between 1970 and 1978. At the time of release Swan Song officials were adamant that this was absolutely the last of the unreleased material. Years later we know this to be more than a little untruth when one considers the material that has subsequently appeared on box sets (three unreleased recordings and Hey Hey What Can I Do), compilations (a couple of DVD video tracks), The BBC Sessions (no less than twenty four tracks!) and the double DVD set (thirty recordings plus a decent number of promotional clips). Not to mention of course the almost uncountable bootleg recordings. Collectors of the bootlegs (mostly vinyl of course in 1982 when Coda was released) were of course well aware of the untruth even back then!

All that aside Coda is actually a great listen and today still sounds extremely fresh. Certainly a more cohesive and balanced album than In Through The Out Door and to many Presence as well. The downside with it was its rather meagre length. Running in at a fraction over thirty-three minutes many were justified to think they had been a little short-changed. Jimmy Page and Co. could have at least added Hey Hey What Can I Do! Actually this would be the perfect album to re-master with a number of the goodies that were never supposed to exist (but have subsequently made the light of day) such as Travelling Riverside Blues and Baby Come On Home. Coda however does remain a welcome (and at the time of release) final statement from the mighty Zep.

WE'RE GONNA GROOVE
(King/Bethea)

Recorded live at the Royal Albert Hall in January 1970 the track is a perfect example of how Led Zeppelin could cover a song and really make it their own. The band often used this little number to open their shows during this early gig period. The band starts this album as they end it, hard and heavy. Jimmy Page's guitars are a joy to mhear on this one. Interestingly the guitars were overdubbed hence the song sounding like there are at least three Jimmy Page's rocking out live on this one.

POOR TOM
(Page/Plant)

Easing the pace somewhat, Poor Tom has a lovely folksy sound that only Led Zeppelin could capture. A perfect example of how this band could use a heavy drum beat, soft acoustic guitars, harmonica and Plant's haunting vocals to wonderful effect. Recorded on May 6th 1970 at Olympic Studio's, London.

I CAN'T QUIT YOU BABY
(Dixon)

One of the classic blues covers from early Zeppelin, originally released on Led Zeppelin I to be precise, the track was a popular showpiece in the band's early live set. This version was recorded September 1st 1970 during sound check at the Royal Albert Hall. The original version is good, this one really shows how the band had matured and gained confidence during the preceding two years. Page and Bonham really stand out on this one. Classic blues, Zeppelin style.

WALTERS WALK
(Page/Plant)

Another rocky number, this time recorded at Stargroves, England on May 15th 1972. Certainly more than filler this number would not have sounded out of place on Houses Of The Holy or Physical Graffiti even if Plant's vocals sounded a little like he might have had them recorded in a fish tank.

Again John Bonham's drumming is topclass and there is a rather cool solo from Jimmy Page.

OZONE BABY
(Page/Plant)

The first of three tracks recorded on November 15th 1978 at Abba's Polar Studios in Stockholm, Sweden where most of In Through The Out Door was laid down. This track was one of three that was destined for an EP only release DARLENE (John Bonham/John Paul Jones/Jimmy Page/ Robert Plant) Robert Plant would often imitate (in his own special way) Elvis Presley during live shows, especially in the early years. Several previous (and rather awful) studio attempts were obvious nods in the King's direction. It was this number that was probably the best attempt by the band. Recorded on November 15th 1978 at Abba's Polar Studio's the track was the second of the three tracks originally slated for release by Led Zeppelin under a pseudonym. This, as we now know never occurred.

BONZO'S MONTREUX
(John Bonham)

Recorded on November 21st 1976 at Mountain Studios in Montreux, Switzerland the track is so obviously a Bonham hand jam. With the master stick basher in full swing the track is a perfect example showcasing the immense skill John Bonham possessed. In almost anyone else's hand this type of track would be little more than album filler. Not so in this case.

WEARING AND TEARING
(Page/Plant)

The third of the tracks supposedly destined for the 'EP' this one was also recorded at Polar Studio's, this time on November 21st 1978 and the track is a classic Zeppelin rocker. John Bonham's drumming really stands out on this one as well and the track is certainly far superior to several that eventually ended up on In Through The Out Door. The band certainly rock out in style on this one. Simple but effective.

LED ZEPPELIN – BBC SESSIONS

Atlantic 7567-83061-2 Released 1997

Original recordings produced by the BBC Compilation and mastering – Jimmy Page Brilliant recordings capturing some of the best of early Led Zeppelin live. Disk one deals mainly with material from Led Zeppelin I and was all recorded in 1969 in a number of BBC locations over a period of months. Disk two is an unedited concert recorded at the Paris Theatre, London on the 1/4/71. This is one of the few concerts of classic Led Zeppelin from such an early period. Material for the Paris Theatre concert is drawn from the bands first four albums. Classic stuff!

DISK ONE

YOU SHOOK ME – recorded for Top Gear 3/3/69 – transmitted on 23/3/69 - original studio recording was on Led Zeppelin I.

I CAN'T QUIT YOU BABY – recorded for Top Gear 3/3/69 – transmitted on 23/3/69 - original studio recording was on Led Zeppelin I

COMMUNICATION BREAKDOWN – recorded for Chris Grant's Tasty Pop Sundae on 16/6/69 – transmitted on 22/6/69 - original studio recording was on Led Zeppelin I

DAZED AND CONFUSED – recorded for Top Gear 3/3/69 – transmitted on 23/3/69 - original studio recording was on Led Zeppelin I

THE GIRL I LOVE SHE GOT LONG BLACK WAVY HAIR – recorded for Chris Grant's Tasty Pop Sundae on 16/6/69 – transmitted on 22/6/69 – Never released as a studio recording.

WHAT IS AND WHAT SHOULD NEVER BE – recorded for Top Gear 24/6/69 transmitted on 29/6/69 - original studio recording was on Led Zeppelin II

COMMUNICATION BREAKDOWN – recorded for Top Gear 24/6/69 – transmitted on 29/6/69 - original studio recording was on Led Zeppelin I

TRAVELLING RIVERSIDE BLUES – recorded for Top Gear 24/6/69 – transmitted on 29/6/69 - original studio recording was not released until the 1990's.

WHOLE LOTTA LOVE – recorded for Top Gear 24/6/69 – transmitted on 29/6/69 - original studio recording was on Led Zeppelin II

SOMETHIN' ELSE – recorded for Chris Grant's Tasty Pop Sundae 16/6/69 – transmitted on 22/6/69 – Never released as a studio recording.

COMMUNICATION BREAKDOWN – recorded for One Night Stand, Playhouse Theatre, London 27/6/69 – transmitted on 10/8/69 - original studio recording was on Led Zeppelin I

I CAN'T QUIT YOU BABY – recorded for One Night Stand, Playhouse Theatre, London 27/6/69 – transmitted on 10/8/69 - original studio recording was on Led Zeppelin I

YOU SHOOK ME – recorded for One Night Stand, Playhouse Theatre, London 27/6/69 – transmitted on 10/8/69 - original studio recording was on Led Zeppelin I

HOW MANY MORE TIMES – recorded for One Night Stand, Playhouse Theatre, London 27/6/69 – transmitted on 10/8/69 - original studio recording was on Led Zeppelin I

DISK TWO

IMMIGRANT SONG – recorded at the Paris Theatre, London 1/4/71 for the BBC In Concert programme – original studio recording was on Led Zeppelin III

HEARTBREAKER – recorded at the Paris Theatre, London 1/4/71 for the BBC In Concert programme – original studio recording was on Led Zeppelin II

SINCE I'VE BEEN LOVING YOU – recorded at the Paris Theatre, London 1/4/71 for the BBC In Concert programme – original studio recording was on Led Zeppelin III

BLACK DOG – recorded at the Paris Theatre, London 1/4/71 for the BBC In Concert programme – original studio recording was on Led Zeppelin IV

DAZED AND CONFUSED – recorded at the Paris Theatre, London 1/4/71 for the BBC In Concert programme– original studio recording was on Led Zeppelin I

STAIRWAY TO HEAVEN – recorded at the Paris Theatre, London 1/4/71 for the BBC In Concert programme – original studio recording was on Led Zeppelin IV

GOING TO CALIFORNIA – recorded at the Paris Theatre, London 1/4/71 for the BBC In Concert programme – original studio recording was on Led Zeppelin IV

THAT'S THE WAY – recorded at the Paris Theatre, London 1/4/71 for the BBC In Concert programme – original studio recording was on Led Zeppelin III

WHOLE LOTTA LOVE (Medley) – Boogie Chillun'/Fixin' to Die/That's Alright Mamma/A Mess Of Blues – recorded at the Paris Theatre, London 1/4/71 for the BBC In Concert programme – original studio recording was on Led Zeppelin II except for Boogie Chillun'/Fixin' to Die/That's Alright Mamma/A Mess Of Blues which have never been recorded or released as a studio recording

THANK YOU – recorded at the Paris Theatre, London 1/4/71 for the BBC In Concert programme – original studio recording was on Led Zeppelin II

HOW THE WEST WAS WON

Atlantic 7567-83587-2 Released 2003

Long awaited live material, which had been excellently recorded by Eddie Kramer on the 25th June 1972 at the LA Forum and the 27th June 1972 at the Long Beach Arena. These recordings really show Led Zeppelin in their middle period at their very best and the recordings certainly compete with most of the bootlegs from the period as far as quality is concerned. Kevin Shirley has mixed the recordings in classic live stereo although there is a special 5.1 surround sound version available as well. All tracks were recorded at the Long Beach Arena unless indicated with an asterix. * This is certainly amongst the best quality live material that has been released on an official release to date.

DISK ONE

LA DRONE (Page/Jones) – At fourteen seconds short this is quite possibly the shortest track known to man woman or dog. Quite obviously a way to get a writer royalty credit in place.

IMMIGRANT SONG (Page/Plant) – originally released on Led Zeppelin III this live version certainly comes across as a very heavy live number.

HEARTBREAKER (Page/Plant/Jones/Bonham) – originally released on Led Zeppelin II Heartbreaker also serves to gives ones ears a bashing in the live version. This segues (rather badly) into Black Dog.

BLACK DOG (Page/Plant/Jones)* - classic rendition of a classic song.

OVER THE HILLS AND FAR AWAY (Page/Plant) – good as a studio song this live rendition really gives it some balls.

SINCE I'VE BEEN LOVING YOU (Page/Plant/Jones) – absolutely perfect is the best way to describe this moving live version of Zeppelin's premier blues track.

STAIRWAY TO HEAVEN (Page/Plant) – following on from Since I've Been Loving You this rendition of Stairway To Heaven also shines. Led Zeppelin at their best.

GOING TO CALIFORNIA (Page/Plant) – better than ever as a live acoustic number. Features wonderful mandolin playing from John Paul Jones.

THAT'S THE WAY (Page/Plant)* - another track that arguably sounds better here than the original studio version.

BRON-YR-AUR STOMP (Page/Plant) – ditto. With the audience participation the track makes you want to get up and stomp.

DISK TWO

DAZED AND CONFUSED (Page)* – medley includes Walter's Walk (Page/Plant)*, The Crunge (Bonham/Jones/Plant/Page)* - rolling in at a little over twenty-five minutes Jimmy Page really struts his stuff with this excellent version of this early Zep classic and using his famous cello bow he really lets fly. Great to hear Walters Walk (or part of it) and even The Crunge excerpts sound reasonably acceptable.

WHAT IS AND WHAT SHOULD NEVER BE (Page/Plant) – this sounds far better (and certainly heavier) than the original studio recording.

DANCING DAYS (Page/Plant) - almost funky this version features excellent offbeat drumming by John Bonham

MOBY DICK (Bonham/Jones/Page)* - John Bonham's showpiece and it actually sounds very good for an extended drum solo (this version runs in at nearly twenty minutes). Moby Dick however is far better to see and hear at the same time (alternate versions on the DVD's)

DISK THREE

WHOLE LOTTA LOVE (Page/Plant/Jones/Bonham/Willie Dixon) * – medley includes Boogie Chillun (John Lee Hooker/Bernard Besman) * / Let's Have A Party (Jerry Leiber)* / Hello Marylou (Gene Pitney)* / Going Down Slow (James B Oden) * - even from the very early days Whole Lotta Love sounded better live – this version is certainly no exception. Robert Plant's vocal cavorting on the rock and roll numbers is exceptional, something he could rarely pull off in his studio recordings. Live he shines, as does Jimmy Page with his guitar licks.

ROCK AND ROLL (Page/Plant/Jones/Bonham) – good as a studio track, live it really has the power to get one rocking and rolling. Simple but effective.

THE OCEAN (Page/Plant/Jones/Bonham)* - the studio version was always a difficult track to listen to. Live it gets a whole new lease of life.

BRING IT ON HOME (Willie Dixon) – medley includes Bring It On Back (Page/Plant/Jones/Bonham)* - good rock and roll start and excellent harmonica from Robert Plant.

> "I'd met Jimmy on sessions before. It was always Big Jim and Little Jim - Big Jim Sullivan and little Jim and myself and the drummer. Apart from group sessions where he'd play solos and stuff like that, Jimmy always ended up on rhythm guitar because he could not read too well."

John Paul Jones

IMPORTANT COMPILATIONS

Compilations for any band are an inevitable marketing opportunity. Some are wonderful additions, others are abominable creations. Led Zeppelin has had surprisingly few compared to most bands of their statue and ilk. This was undoubtedly due to the lock tight grip that Peter Grant their manager exerted on the label and other industry components. There have been a few items of note in recent years and listed here are some of the more important and interesting items that have been unleashed upon the record buying public.

EARLY DAYS - THE BEST OF LED ZEPPELIN

VOLUME ONE
Atlantic 7567-83619-2 Released 2002

Thirteen track Best Of that features tracks from Led
Zeppelin I thru Led Zeppelin IV. It certainly has most of the
tracks one would think should be picked from the early
years although surprisingly Heartbreaker and Gallows Pole
were not included. When The Levee Breaks would have
been a good track to omit from a Best Of. The album does
feature an enhanced CD video track as well, in this case
Communication Breakdown filmed in black and white.
Certainly a cool collection for the car or ipod. The album
has been released separately or as a double pack with
Latter Days.

1. Good Times, Bad Times

2. Babe I'm Gonna Leave You

3. Dazed And Confused

4. Communication Breakdown

5. Whole Lotta Love

6. What Is And What Should Never Be

7. Immigrant Song

8. Since I've Been Loving You

9. Black Dog

10. Rock And Roll

11. The Battle Of Evermore

12. When The Levee Breaks

13. Stairway To Heaven

THE SONG REMAINS THE SAME FILM - DVD AND VHS

Warner Brothers Released 1976 Produced by Jimmy Page. The classic film issued on video and later DVD. Still a good one to watch at three on a Sunday morning after a night out. Classic cinematography by Joe Massot who got little or no credit for the amazing film he started and by and large made. Falling out with Peter Grant at the eleventh hour certainly didn't help his chances of course. That aside no one can take away the skill utilized to capture this band of bands on celluloid. This has certainly become one of the classic rock films from the seventies.

1. Rock And Roll

2. Black Dog

3. Since I've Been Loving You

4. No Quarter

5. The Song Remains The Same

6. The Rain Song

7. Dazed And Confused

8. Stairway to Heaven

9. Moby Dick

10. Heartbreaker

11. Whole Lotta Love

LED ZEPPELIN DOUBLE DVD

Atlantic / Warner Music Vision 0349-70198-2 Released 2003
An absolutely amazing double DVD set! Long awaited and certainly not a disappointment. Anyone who really wants to have a good overview of Led Zeppelin should buy this collection and it sounds amazing on a 5.1 system and a big screen cranked up and played for your neighbours.

DVD 1

Live At The Royal Albert Hall – 1970

Stunningly good early set recorded in colour. This has to be seen to be believed. It's been bootlegged many times over the years as far as the audio is concerned. To see the band in action is a revelation.
Including We're Gonna Groove, I Can't Quit You Baby, Dazed And Confused, White Summer, What Is And Should Never Be, How Many More Times, Moby Dick, Whole Lotta Love, Communication Breakdown, C'mon Everybody, Something Else, Bring It On Home

EXTRAS

Communication Breakdown – promo 1969 – black and white, lip-sync video – same as promo clip used on Early Days. Danmarks Radio – 1969 – black and white - very enlightening early performances. including Communication Breakdown, Dazed And Confused, Babe I'm Gonna Leave You, How Many More Times.

Supershow – 1969 – colour – brilliant early version of Dazed And Confused.

Tous En Scene – 1969 – Apparently the sound and filming for this show is why Led Zeppelin vigorously declined to perform for TV or do many interviews throughout most of their career. One can see why! It's interesting nonetheless. Including Communication Breakdown, Dazed And Confused

DVD 2

Immigrant Song – 1972

Recorded during the Australian tour the clips from this are from a couple of shows, the sound recording from a concert at Long Beach, California the same year. Powerful clip. Madison Square Garden – 1973 – Shot by Joe Massot during the shows ultimately used for the film The Song Remains The Same. These versions are stunning to see cleaned up and interestingly even use bootleg clips at times where the original film was damaged or missing. Including Black Dog, Misty Mountain Hop, Since I've Been Loving You, The Ocean Earls Court – 1975 – The DVD set is worth it for this section alone. Absolutely stunning acoustic performances and then the band boogie on in no uncertain terms with an extended and extremely pleasing version of Trampled Underfoot and an excellent version of In My Time Of Dying. Stairway To Heaven shines! Including Going to California, That's The Way, Bron Yr Aur Stomp, In My Time Of Dying, Trampled Underfoot, Stairway To Heaven

Knebworth – 1979 – Brilliant performances by Zeppelin – this concert footage and recordings are an absolute must have as well. Weirdly it was the last concert on British soil ever. Stunning stuff! Including Rock And Roll, Nobody's Fault But Mine, Sick Again, Achilles Last Stand, In The Evening, Kashmir, Whole Lotta love

LED ZEPPELIN IN THEIR OWN WORDS

JOHN PAUL JONES
(1977)

INTERVIEWED BY STEVEN ROSEN

What was the impetus behind becoming a bass player?

I used to play piano when I was younger, and there was a rock and roll band forming at school when I was 14, but they didn't want a piano player – all they wanted was drums or bass. I thought, "I can't get the drums on the bus", bass looked easy – four strings, no chords, easy – so I took it up. And it was easy; it wasn't too bad at all. I took it up before guitar, which I suppose is sort of interesting. Before I got a real four-string, my father had a ukulele banjo, a little one, and I had that strung up like a bass, but it didn't quite have the bottom that was required. Actually my father didn't want to have to sign a guarantor to back me in the payments for a bass. He said, "Don't bother with it; take up the tenor saxophone. In two years the bass guitar will never be heard of again." I said, "No Dad, I really want one, there's work for me." He said, "Ah, there's work?" And I got a bass right away.

What was your first bass?

Oh, it was a pig; it had a neck like a tree trunk. It was a solid body Dallas bass guitar with a single cutaway. It sounded all right though, and it was good for me because I developed very strong fingers. I had no idea about setting instruments up then, so I just took it home from the shop. I had an amplifier with a 10" speaker – oh, it was awful. It made all kinds of farting noises. And then I had a converted television; you know one of those big old stand-up televisions with the amp in the bottom and a speaker where the screen should be. I ended up giving myself

double hernias. Bass players always had the hardest time because they always had to cope with the biggest piece of equipment. It never occurred to me when I was deciding between that and drums that I'd have to lug a bass amp.

What kind of music were you playing in that first band?

Shadows, Little Richard, Jerry Lee Lewis stuff. I started doubling on piano. We didn't have a drummer at first, because we never could find one. That happened to another bass player, Larry Graham, Sly Stone's bass player. He started off in a band with no drummer, which is how he got that percussive style. You've got a lot to make up for once the lead guitar takes a solo because there's only you left. You've got to make a lot of noise. We got a drummer after a while whom I taught, would you believe? I've never played drums in my life.

That must have definitely had an influence on your playing.

I suppose it must have. I don't like bass players that go boppity boppity bop all over the neck; you should stay around the bottom and provide the end of the group. I work very closely with the drummer; it's very important.

How long did that first band last?

Not very long. I found a band with a drummer. This band also came along with really nice-looking guitars, and I thought, "Oh, they must be great!" They had Burns guitars so I got myself one, too – the one with the three pickups and a Tru-Voice amplifier. We all had purple band jackets and white shoes, and I thought, "This is it, this is the big time." But as soon as I got out of school I played at American Air Force bases, which was good training, plus they always had great records in the jukebox. That was my introduction to the black music scene, when very heavy gentlemen would come up insisting on Night Train eight times an hour.

What was the first really professional band you were in?

It was with Jet Harris and Tony Meehan (bassist and drummer with The Shadows). That was when I was 17, I suppose. And those were the days when they used to scream all the way through the show. It was just like now, really, where you have to make a dash for the limos at the end of the night – make a sort of terrible gauntlet. In the days before roadies you'd have to drag around your own gear, so we all invested in a roadie. We thought we owed it to ourselves, and this bloke was marvellous. He did everything, he drove the wagon, he lugged the gear, he did the lights – the whole thing.

What kind of bass were you using with Harris and Meehan?

Oh, I got my first Fender then. I lusted after this Jazz bass in Lewisham, and it cost me about $250, I think. It was the new one. They'd just changed the controls, and I used that bass up until last (1975) tour, and then she had to go. She was getting unreliable
and rattling a lot, and I just had to leave her home this time.

What followed your working with that band?

I got into sessions. I thought, "I've had enough of the road", bought myself a dog and didn't work for six months. Then I did start up again. I played in other silly bands. I remember that Jet Harris and Tony Meehan band – John McLaughlin joined on rhythm guitar. It was the first time I'd met him and it was hilarious. Here he was sitting there all night going D minor to G to A minor. That was my first introduction to jazz when he came along, because we'd all get to the gig early and have a blow. Oh, that was something, first meeting him. And then I joined a couple of other bands with him for a while, rhythm and blues bands.

Do you remember the first session that you ever did?

No, I don't think so; it was in Decca Number 2 (studio in London). I was late, and I suddenly realised how bad my reading was. There was another bass player there, a standup bass, and I was just there to provide the click. It was nearly my last session.

Who were some of the people you were doing sessions with?

All kinds of silly people: used to do calls with Tom Jones, Cathy Kirby, Dusty Springfield.

The Rolling Stones and Donovan, too, didn't you?

I only did one Stones session, really. I just did the strings – they already had the track down. It was She's a Rainbow. And then the first Donovan session was a shambles, it was awful. It was Sunshine Superman and the arranger had got it all wrong, so I thought, being the opportunist that I was, "I can do better than that" and actually went up to the producer. He came around and said, "Is there anything we can do to sort of save the session?" And I piped up, "Well, look how about if I play it straight?" – because I had a part which went sort of ooowooooo (imitates a slide up the neck) every now and again, and the other bass player sort of did wooooo (imitates downwards slide) down below, and then there was some funny congas that were in and out of time. And I said, "How about if we just sort of play it straight; get the drummer to do this and that?"

How did the session go?

The session came off, and I was immediately hired as the arranger by Mickie Most, whom I loved working with; he was a clever man. I used to do Herman's Hermits and all that. I mean they were never there; you could do a whole album in a day. And it was great fun and a lot of laughs. I did all of Lulu's stuff and all his artists. I did one Jeff Beck single, and he's never spoken to me since. It was Hi Ho Silver Lining. I did the arrangement for it and I played bass. Then we had Mellow Yellow for Donovan, which we argued about for hours because they didn't like my arrangement at all, not at all. Mickie stood by me. He said, "I like the arrangement, I think it's good." It wasn't Donovan – he didn't mind either – but he had so many people around him saying, "Hey, this isn't you." But he sold a couple of a million on it, didn't he?

Was the Hurdy Gurdy Man session when you first met Jimmy Page?

No. I'd met Jimmy on sessions before. It was always Big Jim and little Jim – Big Jim Sullivan and little Jim and myself and the drummer. Apart from group sessions where he'd play solos and stuff like that, Page always ended up on rhythm guitar because he couldn't read too well. He could read chord symbols and stuff, but he'd have to do anything they'd ask when he walked into a session. But I used to see a lot of him just sitting there with an acoustic guitar sort of raking out chords. I always thought the bass player's life was much more interesting in those days, because nobody knew how to write for bass, so they used to say, "We'll give you the chord sheet and get on with it." So even on the worst sessions you could have a little runaround. But that was good; I would have hated to have sat there on acoustic guitar.

How long did you do sessions?

Three or four years, on and off. Then I thought I was going to get into arranging because it seemed that sessions and running about was much too silly. I started running about and arranging about 40 or 50 things a month. I ended up just putting a blank piece of score paper in front of me and just sitting there and staring at it. Then I joined Led Zeppelin, I suppose, after my missus said to me, "Will you stop moping around the house; why don't you join a band or something?" And I said, "There are no bands I want to join, what are you talking about?" And she said, "Well, look, I think it was in Disc, Jimmy Page is forming a group," – he'd just left the Yardbirds – "why don't you give him a ring?" So I rang him up and said, "Jim, how you doing? Have you got a group yet?" He said, "I haven't got anybody yet." And I said, "Well, if you want a bass player, give me a ring." And he said, "All right, I'm going up to see this singer Terry Reid told me about, and he might know a drummer as well. I'll call you when I've seen what they're like." He went up there, saw Robert Plant, and said, "This guy is really something." We started under the name the New Yardbirds because nobody would book us under anything else. We rehearsed an act, an album, and a tour in about three weeks, and it took off. The first time, we all met in this little room just to see if we could even stand each other. It was wall-to-wall amplifiers and terrible, all old. Robert (Plant) had heard I was a session man, and he was wondering what was going to turn up – some old bloke with a pipe? So Jimmy said, "We're all here, what are we going to play?" And I said, "I don't know, what do you know?" And Jimmy

said, "Do you know a number called, The Train Kept a Rollin'? I told him, "No." And he said, "It's easy, just G to A." he counted it out, and the room just exploded, and we said, "Right. We're on, this is it, this is going to work!" And we just sort of built it up from there. Dazed and Confused came in because Jimmy knew that, but I could never get the sequence right for years; it kept changing all the time with different parts, and I was never used to that. I was used to having the music there – I could never remember – in fact, I'm still the worst in the band remembering anything. And the group jokes about it, "Jonesy always gets the titles wrong and the sequences wrong." Even now I have a piece of paper I stick on top of the Mellotron which says: "Kashmir – remember the coda!"

> "I used to play on a bath salts container with wires on the bottom and on a round coffee tin with a loose wire fixed to it to give a snare drum effect. Plus there were always my mum's pots and pans. When I was ten, my mum bought me a snare drum."

John Bonham

What were some of your early amplifiers?

I've used everything from a lousy made-up job, to a great huge top valve (tube) amp. We started off in a deal with Rickenbacker where we had these awful Rickenbacker amps; they were so bad. Our first tour was a shambles. For about a year I never even heard the bass. They said, "We've designed this speaker cabinet for you," and I said, "Let me see it, what's it got in it?" It had one 30" speaker! I said, "All right, stand it up there alongside whatever else I've got, and I'll use it." I plugged it in, and in a matter of five seconds it blew up. I thought the bloke was having me on; I said, "There's no such thing as a 30" speaker!" And I had to take the back off because I couldn't believe it. Then we met the guy from Univox, and he came up with a bass stack, which unfortunately didn't last the night. But while it was going, it was the most unbelievable sound I've ever heard. It was at the Nassau Coliseum in New York, I remember, and the bass filled the hall. It was so big, it couldn't have lasted. I don't think I'll come across anything that sounded like that. But as I said, three numbers and wheel the Acoustics out again. I used two or three 360 standard Acoustics for quite a long time. They served me well.

You used the jazz bass until just recently?

Yeah. Oh, I got ahold of a very nice Gibson violin bass (pictured in the little cut-out wheel on the cover of Led Zeppelin III). That was nice, too, it's not stage-worthy, but it gives a beautiful warm sound. I don't like Gibson basses generally because they feel all rubbery; I like something you can get your teeth into. But the violin bass was the only Gibson that was as heavy as a Fender to play, but still had that fine Gibson sound. I used it on Led Zeppelin III, and I've used it every now and again, usually when I'm tracking a bass after I've done keyboards for the main track. The one I have went through Little Richard's band and then through James Brown's band, and it arrived in England. In fact, I saw it in an old movie clip of Little Richard. It was probably about a '48 or '50 or something

like that; it was the original one. Actually, I've also got an old '52 Telecaster bass. I used that onstage for a while, for Black Dog and things like that.

Do you ever use a pick when you play?

Yes, when the situation demands it; on the eight-string it's awful messy with your fingers. On The Song Remains the Same I use a pick to get that snap out of the instrument. It's fun, you play different. If I was just playing straight bass, I'd use fingers. When I first started I always used my fingers.

How has playing with Jimmy Page for the last nine years styled your playing?

That's hard. I play a lot looser than I used to. For instance, somebody like John Entwistle is more of a lead instrument man than I am. I tend to work closer with Bonzo I think. But then again, I don't play that much bass onstage anymore, what with the pianos and the Mellotron. I'll always say I'm a bass player, though.

How do you develop a bass part?

You put in what's correct and what's necessary. I always did like a good tune in the bass. For example, listen to What is and what should never be (on Led Zeppelin II). The role of a bassist is hard to define. You can't play chords so you have a harmonic role; picking and timing notes. You'll suggest a melodic or harmonic pattern, but I seem to be changing anyway toward more of a lead style. The Alembic bass is doing it; I play differently on it. But I try to never forget my role as a bass player: to play the bass and not mess around too much up at the top all the time. You've got to have somebody down there, and that's the most important thing. The numbers must sound right, they must work right, they must be balanced.

Do you practise?

In a word, no. I fool around on piano but bass I never practise. Although again, with the Alembic, I'm beginning to feel, "Wouldn't it be nice to have it in the room?" It really makes you want to play more, which is fantastic.

Who do you listen to?

I don't. I used to listen to a lot of jazz bass players once, but jazz has changed so much now, it's hardly recognisable. I listened to a lot of tenor sax players: Sonny Rollins, John Coltrane and all those people. Bass players? Scott La Faro, who died. He used to be with
(jazz pianist) Paul Chambers. Ray Brown and Charlie Mingus, of course. I'm not too keen on the lead bass style of some players. Paul McCartney, I've always respected; he puts the notes in the right place at the right time. He knows what he's about.

There's nothing you'd like to do outside of Zeppelin in an instrumental context?

I always get the feeling I'd like to write a symphony. I like all music. I like classical music a lot – Ravel, Bach; of course, Mozart I could never stand, though to play it on the piano is great fun. If Bach had ever come across the bass guitar, he would have loved it. Rock and
roll is the only music left where you can improvise. I don't really know what's happened to jazz; it has really disappointed me. I guess they started playing rock and roll.

So you're able to continually experiment in Zeppelin and expand your playing?

Yes, absolutely. I wouldn't be without Zeppelin for the world.

JIMMY PAGE
INTERVIEWED BY STEVEN ROSEN

Conducting an interview with Jimmy Page, lead guitarist and producer/arranger for England's notorious hard rock band Led Zeppelin, amounts very nearly to constructing a mini-history of British rock and roll itself. Perhaps one of Zeppelin's more outstanding characteristics is its endurance and being able to remain intact (no personnel changes since its inception) through an extremely tumultuous decade involving not only rock, but also popular music in general. Since 1969, the group's four members – Page, bass player John Paul Jones, vocalist Robert Plant and drummer John Bonham – have produced eight albums (two are doubles) of original and often revolutionary compositions with a heavy sound – not metal but plodding and relentlessly driving.

For as long as the band has been an entity, their records, coupled with several well-planned and highly publicised European and American tours, have exerted a profound and acutely recognisable influence on rock groups and Guitar Players on both sides of the Atlantic. Page's carefully calculated guitar frenzy, engineered through the use of controlled distortion and meticulous productions, surrounds Plant's expressive vocals to create a tension and excitement rarely matched by the band's numerous emulators. But the prodigious contributions of James Patrick Page, born on January 9, 1944, in Middlesex, England, date back well in advance of the formation of his present band.

His work as a session guitarist earned him credits so lengthy (some sources cite Jimmy as having played on 50-90% of the records released in the UK during 1963-65) that he is no longer sure of each and every cut on which he played. Even without the exact number of records played on, the range of his interaction as musician and sometimeproducer with the landmark groups and indivuals

Were your parents musical?

No, not at all. But they didn't mind me getting into it; I think that they were quite relieved to see something being done instead of an artwork, which they thought was a loser's game.

What music did you play when you first started?

I wasn't really playing anything properly. I just knew a few bits of solos and things, not much. I just kept getting records and learning that way. It was the obvious influences at the beginning: Scotty Moore, James Burton, Cliff Gallup – he was Gene Vincent's guitarist – Johnny Weeks, later; and those seemed to be the most sustaining influences until I began to hear blues guitarists Elmore James, B.B. King, and people like that. Basically, that was the start: a mixture between rock and blues. Then I stretched out a lot more, and I started doing studio work. I had to branch out, and I did. I might do three sessions a day: a film in the morning, and then there'd be something like a rock band, and then maybe a folk one in the evening. I didn't know what was coming! But it was a really good disciplinary area to work in, the studio. And it also gave me a chance to develop all of the different styles.

Do you remember the first band you were in?

Just friends and things. I played in a lot of different small bands around, but nothing you could ever get any records of. What kind of music were you playing with (early English rock band) Neil Christian and the Crusaders? This was before the Stones happened, so we were doing Chuck Berry, Gene Vincent, and Bo Diddley things mainly. At the time, public taste was more engineered towards Top Ten records, so it was a bit of a struggle. But there'd always be a small section of the audience into what we were doing.

Wasn't there a break in your music career?

Yes, I stopped playing and went to art college for about two years, while concentrating more on blues playing on my own. And then from art college to the (early British rock mecca) Marquee Club in London. I used to go up and jam on a Thursday night with the interlude band. One night somebody said, "Would you like to play on a record?" and I said, "Yeah, why not?" It did quite well, and that was it after that. I can't remember the title of it now. From that point I started getting all this studio work. There was a crossroads: is it an art career or is it going to be music? Well anyway, I had to stop going to the art college because I was really getting into music. Big Jim Sullivan – who was really brilliant – and I were the only guitarists doing those sessions. Then a point came where Stax Records (Memphis-based rhythm and blues label) started influencing music to have more brass and orchestral stuff. The guitar started to take a back trend with just the occasional riff. I didn't realise how rusty I was going to get until a rock and roll session turned up from France, and I could hardly play. I thought it was time to get out, and I did.

You just stopped playing?

For a while I just worked on my stuff alone, and then I went to a Yardbirds concert at Oxford, and they were all walking around in their penguin suits. (Lead singer) Keith Relf got really drunk and was saying "Fuck you" right in the mike and falling into the drums. I thought it was a great anarchistic night, and I went back into the dressingroom and said, "What a brilliant show!" There was this great argument going on; (bass player) Paul Samwell-Smith saying, "Well, I'm leaving the group, and if I was you, Keith, I'd do the very same thing." So he left the group, and Keith didn't. But they were stuck, you see, because they had commitments and dates, so I said, "I'll play the bass if you like." And then it worked out that we did the dual lead guitar thing as soon as (previously on rhythm guitar) Chris Dreja could get it together with bass, which happened, though not for long. But then came the question of discipline.

If you're going to do dual lead guitar riffs and patterns, then you've got to be playing the same things. Jeff Beck had discipline occasionally, but he was an inconsistent player in that when he's on, he's probably the best there is, but at that time, and for a period afterwards, he had no respect whatsoever for audiences.

You were playing acoustic guitar during your session period?

Yes, I had to do it on studio work. And you come to grips with it very quickly too, very quickly, because it's what is expected. There was a lot of busking (singing on street corners) in the earlier days, but as they say, I had to come to grips with it, and it was a good schooling.

You were using the Les Paul for those sessions?

The Gibson 'Black Beauty' Les Paul Custom. I was one of the first people in England to have one, but I didn't know that then. I just saw it on the wall, had a go with it, and it was good. I traded a Gretsch Chet Atkins I'd had before for the Les Paul.

What kind of amplifiers were you using for session work?

A small Supro, which I used until someone, I don't know who, smashed it up for me. I'm going to try to get another one. It's like a Harmony amp, I think, and all of the first album (Led Zeppelin) was done on that.

What do you remember most about your early days with the Yardbirds?

One thing is it was chaotic in recording. I mean we did one tune and didn't really know what it was. We had Ian Stewart from the Stones on piano, and we'd just finished the take, and without even hearing it (producer) Mickie Most said, "Next." I said, "I've never worked like this in my life," and he said, "Don't worry about it." It was all done very quickly, as

it sounds. It was things like that that really led to the general state of mind and depression of Relf and (drummer) Jim McCarty that broke the group up. I tried to keep it together, but there was no chance; they just wouldn't have it. In fact Relf said the magic of the band disappeared when Clapton left (British rock/blues guitarist Eric Clapton played with the Yardbirds prior to Beck's joining). I was really keen on doing anything, though, probably because of having had all that studio work and variety beforehand. So it didn't matter what way we wanted to go; they were definitely talented people, but they couldn't really see the wood for the trees at the time.

You thought the best period of the Yardbirds was when Jeff Beck was with them?

I did, Giorgio Gomelsky (the Yardbirds' manager and producer) was good for him because he got him thinking and attempting new things. That's when they started all sorts of departures. Apparently (co-producer) Simon Napier-Bell sang the guitar riff of Over Under Sideways Down (on LP of the same name) to Jeff to demonstrate what he wanted, but I don't know whether that's true or not. I never spoke to him about it. I know the idea of the record was to sort of emulate the sound of the old Rock around the Clock type record; that bass and backbeat thing. But it wouldn't be evident at all; every now and again he'd say, "Let's make a record around such and such," and no-one would ever know what the example was at the end of the song.

Can you describe some of your musical interaction with Beck during the Yardbirds period?

Sometimes it worked really great, and sometimes it didn't. There were a lot of harmonies that I don't think anyone else had really done, not like we did. The Stones were the only ones who got into two guitars going at the same time from old Muddy Waters records. But we were more into solos rather than a rhythm thing. The point is, you've got to have the parts worked out, and I'd find that I was doing what I was supposed to, while something totally different would be coming from Jeff. That was all right for the areas of improvisation but there were other parts where it just did not work. You've got to understand that Beck and I came from the same sort of roots. If you've got things you enjoy, then you want to do them – to the horrifying point where we'd done our first LP (Led Zeppelin) with You Shook Me, and then I heard he'd done You Shook Me (Truth). I was terrified because I thought they'd be the same. But I hadn't even known he'd done it, and he hadn't known that we had.

Did Beck play bass on Over Under Sideways Down?

No. In fact for that LP they just got him in to do the solos because they'd had a lot of trouble with him. But then when I joined the band, he supposedly wasn't going to walk off anymore. Well, he did a couple of times. It's strange; if he'd had a bad day, he'd take it out on the audience. I don't know whether he's the same now; his playing sounds far more consistent on records. You see on the Beck's Bolero (Truth) thing I was working with that, the track was done and then the producer just disappeared. He was never seen again; he simply didn't come back. (Simon) Napier-Bell just sort of left me and Jeff to it.

Jeff was playing, and I was in the box (recording booth). And even though it says he wrote it, I wrote it. I'm playing the electric 12-string on it. Beck's doing the slide bits, and I'm basically playing around the chords. The idea was built around (classical composer) Maurice Ravel's Bolero. It's got a lot of drama to it; it came off right. It was a good line-up too, with (The Who's drummer) Keith Moon and everything.

Wasn't that band going to be Led Zeppelin?

It was, yeah. Not Led Zeppelin as a name; the name came afterwards. But it was said afterwards that that's what it could have been called. Because Moonie wanted to get out

of The Who, and so did (Who bass player) John Entwistle, but when it came down to getting hold of a singer, it was either going to be (guitarist/organist/singer with English pop group Traffic) Steve Winwood or (guitarist/vocalist with Small Faces) Steve Marriott. Finally it came down to Marriott. He was contacted, and the reply came back from his manager's office: "How would you like to have a group with no fingers, boys?" Or words to that effect. So the group was dropped because of Marriott's other commitment, to the Small Faces. But I think it would have been the first of all those bands sort of like the Cream and everything. Instead it didn't happen – apart from the Bolero. That's the closest it got. John Paul (Jones) is on that too; so is Nicky Hopkins (studio keyboard player with various British rock groups).

You only recorded a few songs with Beck on record?

Yeah. Happenings Ten Years Time Ago (The Yardbirds Greatest Hits), Stroll On (Blow Up), The Train Kept A Rollin' (Having A Rave-up with the Yardbirds), and Psycho Daisies, Bolero and a few other things. None of them were with the Yardbirds but earlier on – just some studio things, unreleased songs: Louie Louie and things like that; really good though, really great.

Were you using any boosters with the Yardbirds to get all those sounds?

Fuzztone which I'd virtually regurgitated from what I heard on 2000 Pound Bee by The Ventures. They had a Fuzztone. It was nothing like the one this guy, Roger Mayer, made for me; he worked for the Admiralty (British Navy) in the electronics division. He did all the fuzz pedals for Jimi Hendrix later; all those octave doublers and things like that. He made this one for me, but that was all during the studio period, you see. I think Jeff had quite a lot of the boost and that sort of sustain in the music.

"John Paul Jones has never worked with anybody like me before - me not knowing anything of the rudiments of music or anything like that and not really desiring to learn them. Its been amazing how we hit it off."

Robert Plant

You were also doing all sorts of things with feedback?

You know, I Need You (Kinkdom) by The Kinks? I think I did that bit there in the beginning. I don't know who really did feedback first; it just sort of happened. I don't think anybody consciously nicked it from anybody else. It was just going on. But Pete Townshend (lead guitarist with The Who) obviously was the one, through the music of his group, who made the use of feedback more his style, and so it's related to him. Whereas the other players like Jeff and myself were playing more single note things than chords.

You used a Danelectro with the Yardbirds?

Yes, but not with Beck. I did use it in the latter days. I used it onstage for White Summer (Little Games). I used a special tuning for that; the low string down to B, then A, D, G, A and D. It's like a modal tuning, a sitar tuning, in fact.

Was Black Mountain Side (done on Led Zeppelin) an extension of that?

I wasn't totally original on that. It had been done to death in the folk clubs a lot; Annie Briggs was the first one that I heard do that riff. I was playing it as well, and then there was (English guitarist) Bert Jansch's version. He's the one who crystallised all the acoustic playing as far as I'm concerned. Those first few albums of his were absolutely brilliant. And the tuning on Black Mountain Side is the same as White Summer. It's taken a bit of battering, the Danelectro guitar, I'm afraid.

You used a Vox 12-string with the Yardbirds, right?

That's right. I can't remember the titles now; the Mickie Most things, some of the Bsides. I remember there was one with an electric 12-string guitar solo on the end of it, which was all right. I don't have copies of them now, and I don't know what they're called. I've got Little Games but that's about it.

You were using Vox amps with the Yardbirds?

AC 30s. They've held up consistently well. Even the new ones are pretty good. I tried some; I got four in and tried them out, and they were all reasonably good. I was going to build up a big bank of four of them, but Bonzo's kit is so loud that they just don't come over the top of it properly.

What kind of guitar were you using on the first Led Zeppelin album?

A Telecaster. I used the Les Paul with the Yardbirds on about two numbers and a Fender for the rest. You see the Les Paul Custom had a central setting, a kind of out-ofphase pickup sound which Jeff couldn't get on his Les Paul, so I used mine for that.

Was the Telecaster the one Beck gave to you?

Yes. There was work done on it but only afterwards. I painted it; everyone painted their guitars in those days. And I had reflective plastic sheeting underneath the pick guard that gives rainbow colours.

It sounds exactly like a Les Paul.

Yeah, well that's the amp and everything. You see, I could get a lot of tones out of the guitar, which you normally couldn't. This confusion goes back to those early sessions again with the Les Paul. Those might not sound like a Les Paul, but that's what I used. It's just different amps, mike placings, and all different things. Also, if you just crank it up to the distortion point so you can sustain notes, it's bound to sound like a Les Paul. I was using the Supro amp for the first album and still do. The Stairway To Heaven solo was done when I pulled out the Telecaster, which I hadn't used for a long time, plugged it into the Supro, and away it went again. That's a different sound entirely from any of the rest of the first album. It was a good versatile setup. I'm using a Leslie on the solo on Good Times Bad Times. It was wired up for an organ thing.

What kind of acoustic guitar are you using on Black Mountain Side and Babe, I'm Gonna Leave You?

That was a Gibson J-200, which wasn't mine; I borrowed it. It was a beautiful guitar, really great. I've never found a guitar of that quality anywhere since. I could play so easily on it, get a really thick sound; it had heavy gauge strings on it, but it just didn't seem to feel like it.

Do you just use your fingers when playing acoustic?

Yes. I used fingerpicks once, but I find them too spiky; they're too sharp. You can't get the tone or response that you would get, say, the way classical players approach gutstring instruments. The way they pick, the whole thing is the tonal response of the string. It seems important.

Can you describe your picking style?

I don't know, really; it's a cross between fingerstyle and flatpicking. There's a guy in England called Davey Graham, and he never used any fingerpicks or anything. He used a thumbpick every now and again, but I prefer just a flatpick and fingers because then it's easier to get around from guitar to guitar. Well, it is for me anyway. But apparently he's got callouses on the left hand and all over the right as well; he can get so much attack on his strings, and he's really good. The guitar on Communication Breakdown sounds as if it's coming out of a shoe box.

Yeah. I put it in a small room, a little tiny vocal booth-type thing and miked from a distance. You see, there's a very old recording maxim which goes, "Distance makes depth". I've used that a hell of a lot on recording techniques with the band generally, not just me. You were always used to them close-miking amps, just putting the microphone in front, but I'd have a mike right out the back as well, and then balance the two, and get rid of all the phasing problems; because really, you shouldn't have to use an EQ in the studio if the instruments sound right. It should all be done with the microphones. But see, everybody has gotten so carried away with the EQ pots that they have forgotten the whole science of microphone placement. There aren't too many guys who know it. I'm sure Les Paul knows a lot; obviously he must have been well into that, well into it, as were all those who produced the early rock records where there were only one or two mikes in the studio.

The solo on I Can't Quit You Baby is interesting – many pulloffs in a sort of sloppy but amazingly inventive style. There are mistakes in it, but it doesn't make any difference. I'll always leave the mistakes in. I can't help it. The timing bits on the A and the B flat parts are right, though it might sound wrong. The timing just sounds off. But there are some wrong notes. You've got to be reasonably honest about it. It's like the film track album (The Song Remains the Same); there's no editing really on that. It wasn't the best concert playingwise at all, but it was the only one with celluloid footage so, there it was. It was all right, it was just one 'as-it-is' performance. It wasn't one of those real magic nights, but then again it wasn't a terrible night. So, for all its mistakes and everything else, it's a very honest film track. Rather than just trailing around through a tour with a recording mobile truck waiting for the magic night, it was just, "There you are – take it or leave it." I've got a lot of live recorded stuff going back to '69.

> " It comes out to 36 hours - I know that because I had to pay the bills! Of course. It wasn't like we went into there for 36 hours non stop, but we paid for 36 hours of studio time. "

Jimmy Page

Jumping ahead to the second album, Led Zeppelin II, the riff in the middle of Whole Lotta Love was a very composed and structured phrase. I had it worked out already before entering the studio. I had rehearsed it. And then all of that other stuff, sonic wave sound and all that, I built it up in the studio, and put effects on it and things, treatments.

How is that descending riff done?
With a metal slide and backwards echo. I think I came up with that first before anybody. I know it's been used a lot now but not at the time I thought of it on this Mickie Most thing. In fact some of the things that might sound a bit odd have, in fact, backwards echo involved in them as well.

What kind of effect are you using on the beginning of Ramble On?
If I can remember correctly, it's like harmony feedback, and then it changes. To be more specific, most of the tracks just start off bass, drums, and guitar and once you've done the drums and bass, you just build everything up afterwards. It's like a starting point, and you start constructing from square one.

Is the rest of the band in the studio when you put down the solos?
No, never. I don't like anybody else in the studio when I'm putting on the guitar parts. I usually just limber up for a while and then maybe do three solos and take the best from the three.

Is there an electric 12-string on Thank You?
Yes. I think it's a Fender or Rickenbacker.

What is the effect on Out on the Tiles?
Now that is exactly what I was talking about: close-miking and distance-miking, that's ambient sound. Getting the distance of the time lag from one end of the room to the

"How can anybody be a 'dated flower child'? The essence of the whole trip was the desire for peace and tranquility and an idyllic situation. That's all anybody could ever want. So how could it be 'dated flower-child gibberish'? If it is, then I'll just carry on being a dated flower child"

Robert Plant

other and putting that in as well. The whole idea, the way I see recording, is to try and capture the sound of the room live and the emotion of the whole moment and try to convey that across. That's the very essence of it. And so, consequently you've got to capture as much of the room sound as possible. On Tangerine, it sounds as if you're playing a pedal steel. I am. And on the first LP there's a pedal steel. I had never played steel before, but I just picked it up. There's a lot of things I do first time around that I haven't done before. In fact, I hadn't touched a pedal steel from the first album to the third. It's a bit of a pinch really from the things that Chuck Berry did. But nevertheless it fits. I use pedal steel on Your Time Is Gonna Come. It sounds like a slide or something. It's more out of tune on the first album because I hadn't got a kit to put it together.

You've also played other stringed instruments on record?

Gallows Pole was the first time for banjo and on The Battle Of Evermore a mandolin was lying around. It wasn't mine, it was Jonesy's. I just picked it up, got the chords, and it sort of started happening. I did it more or less straight off. But you see that's fingerpicking again, going on back to the studio days and developing a certain amount of technique. At least enough to be adapted and used. My fingerpicking is a sort of cross between Pete Seeger, Earl Scruggs and total incompetence.

The fourth album was the first time you used a double-neck?

I didn't use a double-neck on that, but I had to get one afterwards to play Stairway to Heaven.I did all those guitars on it; I just built them up. That was the beginning of my building harmonised guitars properly. Ten Years Gone was an extension of that, and then Achilles' Last Stand is like the essential flow of it really, because there was no time to think the things out; I just had to more or less lay it down on the

first track and harmonize on the second track. It was really fast working on Presence. And I did all the guitar overdubs on that LP in one night. There were only two sequences. The rest of the band, not Robert, but the rest of them I don't think really could see it to begin with. They didn't know what the hell I was going to do with it. But I wanted to give each section its own identity, and I think it came off really good. I didn't think I'd be able to do it in one night; I thought I'd have to do it in the course of three different nights to get the individual sections. But I was so into it that my mind was working properly for a change. It sort of crystallised and everything was just pouring out. I was very happy with the guitar on that whole album as far as the maturity of the playing goes.

When you started playing the double-neck did it require a new approach on your part?

Yes. The main thing is, there's an effect you can get where you leave the 12-string neck open as far as the sound goes and play on the six-string neck, and you get the 12-strings vibrating in sympathy. It's like an Indian sitar, and I've worked on that a little bit. I use it on Stairway like that; not on the album but on the soundtrack and film. It's surprising, it doesn't vibrate as heavily as a sitar would, but nonetheless does add to the overall tonal quality.

You think your playing on the fourth album is the best you've ever done?

Without a doubt. As far as consistency goes and as far as the quality of playing on a whole album, I would say yes. But I don't know what the best solo I've ever done is – I have no idea. My vocation is more in composition really than in anything else. Building up harmonies. Using the guitar, orchestrating the guitar like an army – a guitar army. I think that's where it's at, really, for me. I'm talking about actual orchestration in the same way that you'd orchestrate a classical piece of music. Instead of using brass and violins you treat the guitars with synthesisers or other devices;

give them different treatments, so that they have enough frequency range and scope and everything to keep the listener as totally committed to it as the player is. It's a difficult project, but it's one that I've got to do.

Have you done anything towards this end already?

Only on these three tunes: Stairway to Heaven, Ten Years Gone and Achilles' Last Stand, the way the guitar is building. I can see certain milestones along the way like "Four Sticks," in the middle section of that. The sound of those guitars, that's where I'm going. I've got long pieces written. I've got one really long piece written that's harder to play than anything. It's sort of classical, but then it goes through changes from that mood to really laid-back rock, and then to really intensified stuff. With a few laser notes thrown in, we might be all right.

When was the first time you used the violin bow?

The first time I recorded with it was with the Yardbirds. But the idea was put to me by a classical string player when I was doing studio work. One of us tried to bow the guitar, then we tried it between us and it worked. At that point I was just bowing it, but the other effects I've obviously come up with on my own – using wah-wah, and echo. You have to put rosin on the bow, and the rosin sticks to the string and makes it vibrate.

Do you think when you went from the Telecaster to the Les Paul that your playing changed?

Yes, I think so. It's more of a fight with the Telecaster, but there are rewards. The Gibson's got stereotyped sound maybe, I don't know. But it's got a beautiful sustain to it, and I like sustain because it relates to bowed instruments and everything; this whole area that everyone's been pushing and experimenting in. When you think about it, it's mainly sustain.

Do you use special tunings on the electric guitar?

All the time; they're my own that I've worked out, so I'd rather keep those to myself, really. But they're never open tunings; I have used those, but most of the things I've written have not been open tunings, so you can get more chords into them.

Did you ever meet any of those folk players you admire – Bert Jansch, John Renbourn or any of them?

No, and the most terrifying thing of all happened about a few months ago. Jansch's playing appeared as if it was going down or something, and it turns out he's got arthritis. I really think he's one of the best. He was, without any doubt, the one who crystallised so many things. As much as Hendrix had done on electric, I think he's done on the acoustic. He was really way, way ahead. And for something like that to happen is such a tragedy, with a mind as brilliant as that. There you go. Another player whose physical

handicap didn't stop him is Django Reinhardt. For his last LP they pulled him out of retirement to do it. He'd been retired for years and it's fantastic. You know the story about him in the caravan and losing fingers and such. But the record is just fantastic. He must have been playing all the time to be that good – it's horrifyingly good. Horrifying. But it's always good to hear perennial players like that, like Les Paul, and people like that.

You listen to Les Paul?

Oh, yeah. You can tell Jeff (Beck) did too, can't you? Have you ever heard It's Been a Long, Long Time? (mid-40s single by the Les Paul Trio with Bing Crosby). You ought to hear that. He does everything on that, everything in one go. And it's just one guitar; it's basically one guitar even though they've tracked on rhythms and stuff. But my goodness, the introductory chords and everything are fantastic. He sets this whole tone, and then he goes into this solo which is fantastic. Now that's where I heard feedback first – from Les

Paul. Also vibratos and things. Even before B.B. King, you know, I've traced a hell of a lot of rock and roll, little riffs and things, back to Les Paul, Chuck Berry, Cliff Gallup and all those – it's all there. But then Les Paul was very influenced by Reinhardt, wasn't he? Very much so. I can't get my hands on the records of Les Paul, the Les Paul Trio, and all that stuff. But I've got all the Capitol LPs and things. I mean he's the father of it all: multi-tracking and everything else. If it hadn't been for him, there wouldn't have been anything really.

You said that Eric Clapton was the person who synthesised the Les Paul sound?
Yeah, without a doubt. When he was with the Bluesbreakers, it was just a magic combination. He got one of the Marshall amps, and away he went. It just happened. I thought he played brilliantly then, really brilliantly. That was very stirring stuff.

Do you think you were responsible for any specifc guitar sounds?
The guitar parts in Trampled Underfoot, this guy Nick Kent (British rock journalist), he came out with this idea about how he thought that was a really revolutionary sound. And I hadn't realised that anyone would think it was, but I can explain exactly how it's done. Again it's sort of backwards echo and wah-wah. I don't know how responsible I was for new sounds because there were so many good things happening around that point, around the release of the first Zeppelin album, like Hendrix and Clapton.

Were you focusing on anything in particular on the first Led Zeppelin LP with regards to certain guitar sounds?
The trouble is keeping a separation between sounds, so you don't have the same guitar effect all the time. And that's where the orchestration thing comes in. It's not easy. I've already planned it, it's already there; all the groundwork has

" Without a doubt It's my best work. As far as consistency goes and as far as the quality of playing on a hole album. I would say it was "

Jimmy Page

been done now. And the dream has been accomplished by the computerised mixing console. The sort of struggle to achieve so many things is over. As I said, I've got two things written, but I'll be working in more. You can hear what I mean on Lucifer Rising (soundtrack for the unreleased Kenneth Anger film). You see, I didn't play any guitar on that, apart from one point. That was all other instruments, all synthesisers. Every instrument was given a process so it didn't sound like what it really was – the voices, drones, mantras and even tabla drums. When you've got a collage of say, four of these sounds together, people will be drawn right in because there will be sounds they hadn't heard before. That's basically what I'm into: collages and tissues of sound with emotional intensity and melody and all that. But you know there are so many good people around like John McLaughlin and people like that. It's a totally different thing than what I'm doing.

Do you feel that your playing grows all the time?
I've got two different approaches, like a schizophrenic guitarist, really. I mean onstage is totally different to the way I approach it in the studio, Presence and my control over all the contributing factors to that LP, the fact that it was done in three weeks, and all the rest of it, is so good for me. It was just good for everything really, even though it was a very anxious point, and the anxiety shows group-wise – you know, "Is Robert going to walk again from his auto accident in Greece?" and all that sort of thing. But I guess the solo in Achilles' Last Stand is in the same tradition as the solo from Stairway to Heaven on the fourth LP. It is on that level to me.

"Nineteen years old and never been kissed. I remember it well. It's been a long time. Nowadays we're more into staying in our rooms and reading Nietzsche. There was good fun to be had, you know…"

Robert Plant

ROBERT PLANT
INTERVIEWED BY STEVEN ROSEN

During a series of interviews to promote his first solo album Pictures at Eleven Rosen was briefly able to get Robert Plant to open up on what was then a closed book. These are some of the first words that Robert had to say in retrospect on his days inside the Zeppelin machine.

Could you compare the new album with Zeppelin's first record?

It was just a coming together. Just as Pictures at Eleven is a lot smoother and a lot more sophisticated, the qualities of the first Led Zeppelin album can never be matched, never be equalled and cannot be anymore. Nevertheless, it was a great gelling of all that talent. It was a long time ago, I'm never going to touch that point again. If I can take songs like Reckless Love and Stranger There than Over There, further on from here then I'll be doing myself proud.

Were there times when Led Zeppelin got a little complacent in the material that found its way onto the records?

Not really, I think by the time we got to Houses of the Holy, like Physical Graffiti, all the way down there was a conscientious air about Jimmy's work, Jimmy's catalytic efforts to get everybody moving one way or another and it's remarkable that we kept it going for as many records as we did. Really there wasn't one record that had anything to do with the one before and that's a great credit when there are so many artists who will unconsciously rest on their laurels and say "this is it, this is the way it must be, or this is the only way we know".

We probably grew up together and as we grew up things like All My Love, Darlene, Ozone Baby all got a little bit more contemporary. When we did the track Wearing and Tearing, which came out on Coda, we did that in 1979 and we wanted to put it out as a single on a different label, putting it down by a different artist just to stick it out alongside The Damned and The Sex Pistols. It was so emphatically fresh; if you hadn't known it was us it could have been anybody at all that was young and virile, that we were then supposed not to be.